FAMOUS
ATHEISTS

Their senseless arguments
and how to easily answer them.

FAMOUS
ATHEISTS

Their senseless arguments
and how to easily answer them.

RAY COMFORT

BRIDGE
LOGOS

Alachua, Florida 32615

Bridge-Logos

Alachua, FL 32615 USA

Famous Atheists
by Ray Comfort

Copyright ©2014 Bridge-Logos

Printed in the United States of America.

Library of Congress Catalog Card Number: 2014945475

International Standard Book Number: 978-1-61036-134-7

Unless otherwise indicated, Scripture quotations are taken from the King James Version (public domain). Scripture quotations marked amp are taken from THE AMPLIFIED BIBLE: OLD TESTAMENT. ©1962, 1964 by Zondervan (used by permission); and from the AMPLIFIED BIBLE: NEW TESTAMENT. © 1958 by the Lockman Foundation (used by permission). Scripture quotations marked NASB are taken from the NEW AMERICAN STANDARD BIBLE®, © The Lockman Foundation 1960, 1962, 1963, 1968, 1971, 1972, 1973, 1975, 1977, 1995. Used by permission. Scripture quotations marked NIV are taken from THE HOLY BIBLE: NEW INTERNATIONAL VERSION®. NIV®. Copyright © 1973, 1978, 1984 by Biblica. All rights reserved worldwide. Scripture quotations marked NKJV are taken from the NEW KING JAMES VERSION. © 1982 by Thomas Nelson, Inc. Used by permission. All rights reserved. Scripture quotations marked NLT are taken from the Holy Bible, New Living Translation copyright © 1996, 2004, 2007 by Tyndale House Foundation. Used by permission of Tyndale House Publishers Inc., Carol Stream, Illinois 60188. All rights reserved.

VP 8-21-14

CONTENTS

Chapter 1   The Issue of Faith
and Evolution.   1

Chapter 2   The Evidence for Evolution
and Its Benefits   11

Chapter 3   What Famous Atheists
Believe   23

Chapter 4   More Famous Atheists   43

Chapter 5   Edison, Hitchins, Gates,
Einstein, and Others   53

Chapter 6   The Good Delusion   61

Chapter 7   The Hornet's Nest   73

Chapter 8   The "Science" Guy   85

Chapter 9   Can the Bible Be Trusted? . .   91

Chapter 10 The Emperor
Has No Clones   105

Notes   113

Chapter 1

THE ISSUE OF FAITH
AND EVOLUTION

Before we look at some of the most well-known freethinkers and what they believe about life, it's important to look closely at a major argument put forward by creationists. It is the dispute over whether or not people "believe" in the subject of evolution, as opposed to it being a scientific fact.

Professor Richard Dawkins is arguably the most famous atheist and the leading spokesperson for Darwinian evolution. He is a strong believer in evolution. However, if you ask most atheists if the theory of evolution has anything to do with a belief, they will tell you it doesn't. It's not something that has to be believed. It is a "fact." But let's look at Professor Richard Dawkins's own words, and watch for his use of the word "believe" when it comes to the theory of evolution. He told the *New York Times*, "It is absolutely safe to say that if you meet somebody who claims not to believe in evolution, that person is ignorant, stupid or insane (or wicked)."[1]

So, according to the professor, if you don't "believe" in evolution, you are ignorant, stupid, insane, or wicked. He would like everyone to believe in the theory. As far as he is concerned, to believe it is to be on the side of true science.

But according to *The New Yorker* (in 2012), "The percentage of Americans that believe in biological evolution has only increased by four percentage points over the last twenty years."[2] Notice again the use of the word "believe."

Back in June 2012, a Gallup poll found that 46 percent of Americans believed God created man, 32 percent believed humans evolved with God's guidance, and 15 percent believed in evolution alone.[3] So the percentage of believers in evolution alone was a mere 15 percent and had only increased by 4 percent in twenty years.

But Richard Dawkins is a believer to a point of *never* doubting. He said, "Evolution is a fact, beyond reasonable doubt, beyond serious doubt, beyond sane, informed, intelligent doubt, beyond doubt evolution is a fact."[4]

The reason he is a believer without doubts is that his convictions rest on his beliefs about fossils, dating processes, and on other theories. When asked the question, "Is atheism the logical extension of believing in evolution?" he didn't correct the questioner and say that it wasn't a belief. Instead he answered, "They clearly can't be irrevocably linked because a very large number of theologians believe in evolution. In fact, any respectable theologian of the Catholic or Anglican or any other sensible church believes in evolution.[5] Similarly, a very large number of evolutionary scientists are also religious. My personal feeling is that understanding evolution led *me* to atheism."[6] So, it was Dawkins's faith in evolution that gave him understanding, and that led him to believe that there was no God.

If we want to understand the laws of physics, we have to first *believe* what we read about physics. We have to have faith in what we read. Faith is the first step to understanding. We can't understand anything scientifically if we don't *believe* that data. But believing in evolution doesn't make it true.

BUT ISN'T EVOLUTION OBSERVABLE?

The University of California–Berkeley addresses what they see as a "misconception" that the theory of evolution is not observable:

> This misconception encompasses two incorrect ideas: (1) that all science depends on controlled laboratory experiments, and (2) that evolution cannot be studied with such experiments. First, many scientific investigations do not involve experiments or direct observation. Astronomers cannot hold stars in their hands and geologists cannot go back in time, but both scientists can learn a great deal about the universe through observation and comparison. In the same way, evolutionary biologists can test their ideas about the history of life on Earth by making observations in the real world.[7]

Surely with such an important question they

have at least one example of what it is that evolutionary biologists observe in the real world. But they don't give one, because there isn't anything that can be observed without making assumptions that are based on belief of data. UC Berkeley continues:

> Second, though we can't run an experiment that will tell us how the dinosaur lineage radiated, we *can* study many aspects of evolution with controlled experiments in a laboratory setting. In organisms with short generation times (e.g., bacteria or fruit flies), we can actually observe evolution in action over the course of an experiment. And in some cases, biologists have observed evolution occurring in the wild. To learn more about rapid evolution in the wild, visit our news story on climate change, our news story on the evolution of PCB-resistant fish, or our research profile on the evolution of fish size in response to our fishing practices. To learn more about the nature of science, visit the Understanding Science website.[8]

They give examples of this "rapid evolution" (evolution that takes place very quickly) by speaking of animals within their own kind "evolving" in the last twenty-five years to climate change. These are not examples of observable Darwinian evolution. This is simply "adaptation" within kinds that happens throughout nature. Fish adapting to their environment are not examples of Darwinian evolution because the fish are not changing "kinds." They are still fish.

Many who believe in evolution also point to all the different "species" of dogs as evidence of evolution, when they are not evidence. There is only one dog kind, and within that kind there are many species—from the tiniest of canines to the Great Dane. No evolution (change of kinds) takes place. It is just an example of variations within the kind.

I was speaking recently to a group of university students, and when I said that I didn't believe in evolution—that it was unscientific and unobservable—an atheist called out, "But what about the tailbone?" The human tailbone is said to be vestigial—that is, it's an evolutionary leftover proving that we are related to primates. However, it's not a "tailbone." It's the coccyx, "the last of five regions of the spine," and it anchors twelve muscles that help us go to the bathroom:

> The tailbone derived its name because some people believe it is a 'leftover' part from human evolution, though the notion that the tailbone serves no purpose is wrong. The coccyx is an extremely important source of attachment for tendons, ligaments, and muscles, though it is structured quite differently than other parts of the spine.[9]

He then called out, "What about the

appendix?" I then explained that the appendix, like the "tailbone," isn't vestigial in the slightest. It's tied in with the human immune system. Duke University, in an article titled, "Appendix Isn't Useless at All: It's a Safe House for Bacteria," tells us that, "long denigrated as vestigial or useless, the appendix now appears to have a reason to be—as a 'safe house' for the beneficial bacteria living in the human gut."[10]

WHAT, THEN IS OBSERVABLE?

A believer in evolution wrote this:

> I am amazed each time I read that some give legitimacy to creationism. Evolutionary biology is a science. Science tries to disprove itself. Creationism is static; it cannot be proven or disproved. It does not qualify for any scientific method of thought or logic. It is not science. Not one person on this earth can prove that any part of the creationist's mythos has ever existed. Faith without proof is a folly. You know you cannot prove creationism, so you deny or subtract from science. Keep your faith, but don't try to legitimize creationism other than what it is, a story.[11]

Recently, a man in New Zealand died after he was horrifically attacked and eaten by a shark. The atheist, however, can't blame God for creating the shark, because he has no belief in God. He has to say that this tragedy was the cold result of the evolutionary process. It was a matter of survival of the fittest. The shark simply ate a primate who was in his territory. The Christian, however, has a different worldview. This terrible death of a human being confirms that we live in a "fallen" creation, under the curse of Genesis—where sharks devour people. So do lions and tigers. Snakes kill, bees sting, mosquitoes suck blood and spread disease, crocodiles bite your arm off, and bears rip open your rib cage. There are a whole lot of other nasty predators that will eat you for dinner, if you get into their territory or if they are hungry enough to come into yours. While evolution rests on faith because the believer has to believe what he's been told about old bones, theories, and dating data, we can "observe" Genesis 1 in the existing creation and in the fossil record. It's all readily observable in nature. Faith isn't needed.

The book of Genesis tells us that all humanity traces itself back to one man. This is the conclusion of modern science.[12] Scripture also says that male and female were created in all the "kinds," and in nature we see that, except for a few hermaphroditic lowlifes, everything has male and female. Horses, cows, dogs, cats, elephants, giraffes, fleas, fish, kangaroos, polar bears, and people all have male and female. That's what the Bible says, and that's what we observe in nature and in the fossil record. Genesis tells us that each of these kinds would reproduce after its own kind, and that's what we see in nature. Dogs reproduce dogs, cats reproduce cats, horses reproduce horses, etc. Nothing reproduces a different kind. There are variations within kinds, such as tiny dogs and Great Danes, but each variation is restricted to the dog "kind." Science tells us: "We all know that elephants only give birth to little elephants, giraffes to giraffes, dogs to dogs and so on for every type of living creature. But why is this so? The answer lies in a molecule called deoxyribonucleic acid (DNA), which contains the biological instructions that make each species unique. DNA, along with the instructions it contains, is passed from adult organisms to their offspring during reproduction."[13]

Genesis accounts for reproduction within kinds.

EVERY ETHNIC GROUP

The book of Genesis also tells us that God made us with knowledge of right and wrong—a sense of guilt when the moral Law (the Ten Commandments) is transgressed. That intuitive morality is observable in every ethnic group, both historically and contemporarily. Every human group has a sense of justice and requires some sort of retribution for crime. Genesis says that death came to all of nature because of the rebellion of the first man—birds, fish, plants, and human beings would all be under the curse of the Creator, and that's what we see both in the fossil record and in the whole of nature. Nothing in nature survives. Everything that was once alive is dead, and everything that is living is dying and will die.

Genesis also says that we live in a *fallen* creation. While we have the warmth of the life-giving sun, the deep blue ocean, an amazing variety of beautiful birds, breathtaking sunsets and sunrises, thousands of succulent fruits, a vast array of colors, beauty, life, love, and laughter, we also have the horror of cancer and thousands of other terrible diseases, killer earthquakes, terrible tornados, endless suffering, and death. Genesis 3 tells us of the "fall" of man, and it is a sad reality we observe daily.

From that point on, the Bible speaks of man as being sinful, and it tells us how evil entered the human race. Watch, read, and listen to today's news. You will observe hundreds of stories of murder, rape, lies, extortion, hatred, greed, adultery, lust, envy, jealousy, anger, and theft. All these things are observable. None of them needs the exercising of any faith. What we see both in natural surroundings and in human nature line up perfectly with what we are told in Genesis. But what we are told about evolution doesn't line up with what we see in nature. While evolutionists would have us believe that everything evolved and is still evolving,[14] there are no dogs or birds or plants that we can observe that are in the process of evolution. Everything is in a state of functional maturity. After it was made, everything was "finished," as Genesis 2:1 says. We don't observe anything dying because it has half a mouth and can't eat, or has a semi-evolved stomach and can't digest, or flies in a circle because it has only one partly evolved wing, or drowns because it has semi-evolved gills. Anything that is said to be observable when it comes to Darwinian evolution is conjecture, and that needs the exercise of faith.

In the next chapter we will look at the evidence for evolution.

Chapter 2

THE EVIDENCE FOR EVOLUTION AND ITS BENEFITS

Darwinian evolution is based on whether or not you *believe* what you've been told about evidence, and "faith is the great cop-out, the great excuse to evade the need to think and evaluate evidence," as Richard Dawkins so eloquently said.[1] So let's take the time to evaluate the evidence.

National Geographic once asked the professor, "What evidence is there to prove that evolution and Darwin were right?"[2] This was his opportunity to provide empirical proof—to silence those who don't believe in evolution. He replied by saying what almost every believer says when pressed for proof—that there is a *mass* of evidence—and that's how he began his answer.

"Many pieces of evidence show that evolution is right," he said, then added, "I'll single out just two. The first is the distribution of animals across the globe. They are exactly as you'd expect them to be if evolution occurred. If you go to Australia all the mammals, save for one or two introduced by man, are marsupials [they have pouches]. Why are they all there and not in Asia too? It's exactly as you'd expect if animals evolved. It's not the way it would be if God had gone around creating animals."[3]

That's "proof" that evolution is true? Australia

has kangaroos, and Asia doesn't. This is his empirical, undeniable, undisputed, observable evidence for the theory of evolution. Here is his second-best shot at providing proof: "Secondly, if you look comparatively at all animals, especially bio-chemically: if you look at molecules in how they differ from animal to animal, or plant to plant, you find a hierarchical [an ordered] pattern of resemblance, which only makes sense if you assume that it's a family tree, a pedigree. Everything—all the evidence—points to evolution."[4]

So here's the twofold proof for the evolutionary theory, according to Dawkins: animals and plants have different molecules—and there are no kangaroos in Asia. It was Carl Sagan who rightly said, "Extraordinary claims require extraordinary evidence."[5] Again, the extraordinary claim that everything evolved from a singularity has no observable evidence, unless you have faith. If you think about it, evolution is about turning untested belief into unshakable truth through the power of institutions and the passage of time. Learning institutions push belief as fact onto students, making the unbelievable believable, because they say that evolution requires a long passage of time. It is understandable for skeptics to say of evolution, "I don't believe in evolution for the same reasons I don't believe in Mother Goose."[6]

The burden of proof lies with the believer in evolution—he believes; I don't. So I continually ask those who believe in evolution for evidence. This answer is typical:

> Let's say you have two giraffes, one giraffe has a rather short neck as the other giraffe has a longer neck, these two giraffes will go on and try to survive by eating from trees, however the short-necked giraffe may not get his daily intake of nutrition and may not be tall enough to eat the required amount of food it needs to survive. So this giraffe will most likely die off, whereas the giraffe with the long neck has no issues with eating and can survive rather well since the giraffe is more adapted to its environment. When the short-neck giraffe dies off it will not have reproduced, meaning there will be no giraffes with its genetic code, but the long-necked giraffe will have reproduced and will have more long-necked giraffe babies, over hundreds or thousands of years the giraffes' necks will keep getting longer and longer because the short-necked giraffes simply die off while the long-necked giraffes tend to thrive.[7]

The giraffe-growing-a-longer-neck theory came from a French scientist named Jean-Baptiste Lamarck at the beginning of the nineteenth century. He believed that a characteristic that is used more and more by an organism becomes bigger and stronger, and one that is not used will eventually disappear. Any characteristic of an organism that improved through use was then passed on to its offspring. This is what he said about the long necks of the giraffe:

1. a giraffe stretches its neck to reach food high up.
2. the giraffe's neck gets longer because it's used a lot.
3. the giraffe's offspring inherit its long neck.[8]

However, the BBC's Bitesize (Science) web page says, "Lamarck's theory was eventually discredited because acquired characteristics do not have a genetic basis. In addition, his theory cannot account for all the observations made of life on Earth. For instance, it would predict that all organisms gradually become complex, and simple organisms disappear."[9]

THE BIG BENEFITS OF ATHEISM

Believing in atheistic evolution does have immense benefits. If we are actual apes, as Mr. Dawkins believes,[10] and there's no heaven or hell and the Bible is bogus, then there's no ultimate right or wrong. That means *anything* that society deems acceptable behavior is allowed. Safe premarital sex is to be encouraged. Protected homosexual sex is morally okay. So is adultery, and pornography. Prostitution should be encouraged, and brothels should be safe, clean—and legal.

Atheistic evolution opens up a whole new exciting world of delirious, guilt-free sexual pleasure for the believer. No wonder Richard Dawkins is so popular. No wonder thousands with raging hormones so love him and sit as his feet, lapping up every word as though it were the gospel truth. What he preaches isn't really about evolution—it's about the *implications* that come with it if it's true. Hugh Hefner prepared the way by making pornography more acceptable in society, and Richard Dawkins became the savior from any moral restraint imposed on us by God. He's this generation's Pied Piper, and he's playing the tune they love to hear.

The Nonbelief of the Atheist

Atheists think Christians are weak because they have "faith." So this should please them. Never have faith in an atheist. Don't trust them for a second. This is because they are not worthy of your trust. Let me give you an example of how much integrity atheists have. I once wrote a book called *You Can Lead an Atheist to Evidence, but You Can't Make Him Think*. When it was first published, it was so popular it knocked Richard Dawkins's book off the number one spot on Amazon.com. Atheists panicked and immediately conspired to pull down the book's ratings. And they certainly did. More than two hundred of them rushed in and gave it a one- or two-star rating, making out that they had read the book and saying that it was far worse than finding a six-inch horse hair in your peanut butter sandwich (disgusting thought). They were told not to make the conspiracy obvious, but they were about as subtle as an elephant standing on a ballerina's foot.[11]

Always keep in mind that atheism's worldview allows them to lie through their atheist teeth. This is because they are desperately fearful of Christianity. Again, the issue here isn't evolution or the existence of God. It's about independence and the pleasure of guilt-free sexual sin. Christianity threatens that freedom by saying that fornication and lust are morally wrong, and that God will hold those who participate accountable. So they fight the light with all their might and will hold back at nothing in their attempts to extinguish it.

THE INCENTIVE

A father of two who was deep in debt to his local bank was once sitting on a New York subway train. For no fault of his own, he was laid off, couldn't meet his mortgage, and had lost his suburban home. He was then forced to rent a house in a bad part of town, and now his youngest was being bullied, and the older boy was into a drug-infested gang and was threatening his mother, who was nightly in tears and even fearful for her life. It looked as though the man would now lose his low-paying job. He had once considered himself to be the happiest man on earth, but was now being plagued with depression and thoughts of suicide.

Suddenly his eye caught sight of a small, black,

leather bag below a seat in the empty carriage. He picked it up, opened it, and to his absolute delight, found what turned out to be $860,000 in hundred dollar bills. On the side of the bag were the embossed words *American Trust Bank, 173 Wall Street.* This was the main branch of the bank to which he owed his mortgage! His worries were suddenly over. He would pay off the loan and its interest, move to a new home in a good neighborhood, take his family on a luxury cruise, and have enough money left over to buy a new car for himself and one for his wife.

Here's my question. What *incentive* did the man have to return the money to its rightful owner? Not much. His motivation to keep it or return it comes down to his character. Does he have the integrity to do that which is right, or should he consider his own happiness and the happiness of his beloved family as having priority? Which is more important to him—happiness or righteousness?

He could easily justify keeping the money. No one would know he found it. The bank didn't need it. Bankers were rich and greedy, and he and his much-loved family desperately needed the money to survive. But there was a problem. He was plagued by the nagging voice of his conscience, and it wouldn't go away.

That night he did research on the legalities of keeping money that had been lost. To his dismay he discovered that he was legally bound to return it. Keeping lost money when the owner was known was considered theft, and if he was caught, he would spend years in prison. As much as he didn't want to, he decided to take the money to the bank and hand it in.

To his amazement, the "greedy" bankers weren't greedy at all. They were so delighted that he'd done the right thing that they freely forgave him the mortgage debt, and rewarded him with $50,000.

Here now is my point. Sexual sin gives delirious joy to red-blooded human beings. No matter what problems sit on our shoulders, no matter how depressed we may be, the fulfillment of lust gives us instant pleasure. The person who coined the phrase "as miserable as sin" was either blind or he was lying. This is the biblical teaching about the pleasure sin gives: "By faith Moses, when he became of age, refused to be called the son of Pharaoh's daughter, choosing rather to suffer affliction with the people of God *than to enjoy the passing pleasures of sin*" (Hebrews 11:24–25 NLT, emphasis added). Sin scratches where we frustratingly itch.

The person who chooses to become an atheist has found unending pleasure in his independence. If he so desires, he can fornicate and indulge in pornographic and sexual imaginations. It has put some spice into his rather mundane life. Why, then, would he consider giving it up? There's no incentive to do so, especially in the light of Professor Richard Dawkins and other intellectuals telling him that anything goes, because we are just primates and there's no God, no heaven, and no hell. Besides, the atheist has the belief that no one knows about the secret pleasures he has found.

So an atheist who believes in the theory of evolution doesn't have any motivation to investigate and see if what he has been told is true. But more than that, he doesn't want it to not be true, and has a strong incentive to justify his lifestyle. So he searches atheist books and websites and cuts and pastes so-called contradictions and inconsistencies in the Bible. He finds accusations that the Bible advocates slavery, mass murder, and genocide; that it has two accounts of creation and differing days on which Adam died; that it asks where Noah put all the animals; that God encourages rape, etc. All these "errors" are like manna from heaven because they strengthen his conviction that there is no Judgment Day or awaiting hell. They fortify his sinful and very pleasurable lifestyle.

But like the father who found the money in the train, there are two problems for the atheist. One is the voice of his conscience. He can dull it, but its accusations will never go away, and second, God's moral law tells him that when he is caught, he is going to end up in God's prison—a place called hell, and there's no chance of parole.

But here's what the atheist doesn't understand. The image he has of God is mistaken. The One for whom he has such a contempt that he denies His very existence—and uses His name to cuss—isn't anything like He is conceived to be. *The Banker is not evil.* He is incredibly kind, rich in mercy, and He will freely forgive all the sin-debt of those who repent and trust the Savior. But more than that, He promises to reward those who trust Him with everlasting life and with pleasure forevermore. He does this, not because we deserve it, but solely because He is good and kind.

DOES GOD ENCOURAGE RAPE?

I was speaking at UC Berkeley back in November 2012, when an atheist stepped up to the open microphone and said that the God I believed in condoned rape. He pointed to Deuteronomy 22:28–29 where, according to him, if a man raped a woman, all he had to do was pay a fine and then marry her. He was angry. This proved that the God of Christianity despised women and was therefore a tyrannical misogynist. Here's the passage: "If a man find a damsel that is a virgin, which is not betrothed, and lay hold on her, and lie with her, and they be found; then the man that lay with her shall give unto the damsel's father fifty shekels of silver, and she shall be his wife; because he hath humbled her, he may not put her away all his days."

These verses don't seem to be speaking of rape, because of the words, "and if they be found," which seems to mean that it was consensual. If "they" were found is a reference to both of them being discovered, and that would then make the required dowry and betrothal make sense. This was similar to what we would nowadays call a "shotgun" (forced) wedding. Add to this thought that the previous verses speak clearly of rape (saying if the man "forces her"), and prescribes capital punishment to the rapist: "But if a man finds a betrothed young woman in the countryside, and the man forces her and lies with her, then only the man who lay with her shall die" (v. 25).

The death sentence for the rapist shows that God cares a great deal about women being validated. But the student didn't seek out the truth, because he had no incentive to do so. He wanted to find some dirt on the Judge.

Chapter 3

WHAT FAMOUS ATHEISTS BELIEVE

Billy Joel: William Martin "Billy" Joel is a talented pianist, singer-songwriter, and a brilliant composer. His first hit was "Piano Man," which hit the charts way back in 1973.

Newsmax said of him:

> The singer publicly broached the topic early in his career, saying during an interview that he is an atheist and positing that religion is a source of many of the world's problems. Then he told *Billboard* magazine in 1994, "I still feel very much like an atheist in the religious aspects of things," but added, "There are spiritual planes I'm aware of that I don't know anything about and that I can't explain."[1]

Billy once said:

> As an atheist you have to rationalize things. You decide first of all that you will not ask Daddy—meaning God in all of his imagined forms—for a helping hand when you're in a jam. Then you have to try and make some sort of sense out of your problems. And if you try and find you can't, you have no choice but to be good and scared—but that's okay! When

animals are afraid, they don't pray, and we're just a higher order of primate. Mark Twain, a great atheist, said it best in *The Mysterious Stranger*, when he stated in not so many words, "Who are we to create a heaven and hell for ourselves, excluding animals and plants in the bargain, just because we have the power to rationalize?"[2]

If Billy likes to rationalize things, I would like him to tell me what he would think of my intellectual capacity if I said I thought he didn't compose "Piano Man," if I believed that it didn't have a composer. It just happened. It was a melodic accident. Such a thought is ludicrous. Every song has a composer, every book has an author, every car has a maker, every painting has a painter, and every building has a builder. So it isn't irrational to take this simple logic a little further and say that nature must have had a Maker. It would be irrational to believe that it made itself. It's more than irrational; it's scientifically impossible. For nature to make itself, it would have had to be preexistent before it made itself.

If I ever had the honor of having lunch with Billy, I would ask him two questions. The first isn't that important, but I would like to know the answer. How does he know that animals don't pray? Does he have some sort of unique access to animal thought-life? The second would be to correct a misunderstanding that is common in atheist circles. Why would he believe that Mark Twain was a "great atheist," when he clearly did believe in the existence of God (something we will look at in a future chapter)?

Brad Pitt: Brad Pitt's faith that God doesn't exist wavers a little. He said, "I oscillate between agnosticism and atheism."[3] Sometimes he's an atheist; other times he's not. He said, "I don't think anyone really knows. You'll either find out or not when you get there, until then there's no point thinking about it."[4]

What Brad says makes sense, if you don't think about it. But if you *do* give some serious thought to his words, they are a little thoughtless. This is why. Billions of people think there *is* a point in thinking about it. They are Hindus, Buddhists, Muslims, Christians, or a hundred and one offshoots of these religions. They think about it because they realize that there's an elephant in the human room, and it holds its crushing foot above the heads of every one of us. It took a full twenty years before I noticed the shadow of its ugly foot.

So the point in thinking about it is that God is eternal and He is the source of all life. If there's an answer to the biggest problem we all have, it is in God and God alone. Not believing that there was a Creator, as Sir Isaac Newton so aptly said, is "senseless."[5] But back to Brad Pitt.

According to *Extra*, Mr. Pitt said that he "got brought up being told things were God's way, and when things didn't work out it was called God's plan."[6] He also said, "I grew up being told God is going to take care of everything and it doesn't always work out that way. And then you're told 'Well, it's God's will.' I got my issues. Man, you don't want to get me started."[7]

If I could have a meal with Brad Pitt, I would also ask him to let me take him through a few of the Ten Commandments to show him that he is in great danger. The applicable analogy would be a man who is standing at the door of a plane, ten thousand feet above the ground. He refuses to put on a parachute because he believes he will find out if he needs it *after* he jumps, and until that time there's no point in thinking about it. To begin thinking about it is the seed that can grow into understanding the truth that Jesus Christ has "abolished death, and brought life and immortality to light through the gospel" (2 Timothy 1:10 NKJV).

George Harrison: George Harrison was known as the quiet Beatle. Quiet people are often quiet because they are deep thinkers. Even though he professed to be an atheist back in 1966, George later wrote, "I want to find God. I'm not interested in material things, this world, fame—I'm going for the real goal."[8] The quiet Beatle had tasted fame and the false security that money brings, but it wasn't the real goal in his life . . . God was. This is because thinkers know that God is the source of all life, and if we want to find everlasting life, we have to somehow get in contact with the Creator. So George became a Hare Krishna and spent much of his life chanting the name of his deity.

I recently spoke with a Hare Krishna who told me that I had to chant God's name if I wanted everlasting life. I told him that as a Christian I already had everlasting life and didn't need to *do* anything. It was a free gift of God. To explain what I meant, I told him that all the great religions outside of Christianity have one thing in common. They are "works righteousness" based; that is, they all maintain that we have to *do* something to find salvation (everlasting life)—we must pray, fast, do good deeds, lie on beds of nails or sit on hard pews, face a certain direction, or eat certain foods.

But here is an eye-opener: *none of that will work*. The Bible tells us that if we lust, we commit adultery in our hearts. If we lie or steal or blaspheme or even just hate someone (the same as committing murder), we are criminals in God's eyes—having violated His moral Law, and are on our way to His prison—a terrible place call hell, and there will be no parole. That means that any "good" works we offer God aren't good works at all. They are an attempt to bribe God, and the One the Bible calls the Judge of the Universe will not be bribed. The only thing that can save us from the wrath of eternal justice is God's mercy.

George Harrison said, "Once I chanted the Hare Krishna mantra all the way from France to Portugal nonstop. I drove for about twenty-three hours and chanted all the way."[9] But to think that we can be forgiven by chanting God's name is like a guilty and deluded criminal repeating, "Judge, judge, judge, judge," and thinking that the judge will somehow be impressed and therefore dismiss his case. No, the only way we can be saved is to have a Savior.

Two thousand years ago, the Creator came to this earth in the form of a Man, suffered for our sins on a wooden cross, and then defeated death. So if a Hindu, Buddhist, Muslim, or Jew (or whoever) wants everlasting life as a free gift from God, all he or she needs to do is repent and trust in the Savior—Jesus Christ. That's the best news this dying world could ever hope to hear.

George Carlin: It takes both courage and talent to stand up in front of fellow human beings and make them crack a smile, and at the same time keep it clean. George Carlin was well-known and loved for what is often known as "black humor," as well as his routines on politics, religion, and various other taboo subjects.

George was a devout atheist. However, like almost every atheist, his concept of God was unbiblical. He said, "Religion easily has the best b***sh** story of all time. Think about it. Religion has convinced people that there's an invisible man . . . living in the sky."[10] I don't know any Christians who believe that God is "an invisible man living in the sky." God is nothing like a man.

Perhaps Carlin had that thought because the Bible says that God made man "in His own image" (Genesis 1:27 NKJV). However, that simply means that God created us with the attributes of His own character. Man is unique in creation because he has a sense of justice and truth. We spend billions of dollars each year to set up court systems to see that justice is done, and we build prisons for those who transgress the laws we enact.

We have other unique attributes that separate us from the animal kingdom. A dog may wag his tail, but he has no evident sense of humor. If you disagree, tell him a funny joke and see if he cracks a smile. Neither does he of his own volition tap his foot to music, or appreciate the splendor of a sunrise or the beauty of a flower. He thinks, reasons, plays, and communicates, but he isn't aware of his "being," as we humans are. "To be, or not to be?" isn't the big question for a dog. But for a human being, to be (to live) or not to be (to die)? is the biggest of all questions.

After creating his nonexistent man in the sky, Mr. Carlin said that this man "watches everything you do every minute of every day. And the invisible man has a list of 10 specific things he doesn't want you to do. And if you do any of these things, he will send you to a special place, of burning and fire and smoke and torture and anguish for you to live forever, and suffer, and burn, and scream, until the end of time. But he loves you. He loves you. He loves you and he needs money."[11]

No doubt that routine produced the desired laughter, but it was just a routine. It wasn't based on truth. The Bible does say that there are things God does not want us to do (the Ten Commandments), and that those who murder, rape, and otherwise transgress His perfect Law will suffer punishment in a terrible place called hell. (See Exodus 20:1–17; Revelation 21:8.) To say that there is no ultimate justice is to say that Hitler and every other mass murderer got away with murder. Such a thought makes God unjust, when He is both just and merciful to all who call upon Him for mercy. So I guess atheism, in the minds of some, deals with that whole dilemma.

Penn Jillette: It was Penn Jillette who said, "Believing there's no God stops me from being solipsistic."[12] A solipsistic person is an extreme skeptic. F.H. Bradley explained the solipsistic view when he said, "I cannot transcend experience, and experience is my experience. From this it follows that nothing beyond myself exists."[13] So according to Mr. Jillette, atheism has stopped him from being closed-minded—no doubt like those who have a belief in the existence of God. It's like a person who believes the sun exists is closed-minded to the thought that it doesn't exist.

But Penn Jillette is beyond being an atheist. He said, "I believe that there is no God. I'm beyond atheism. Atheism is not believing in God. Not believing in God is easy—you can't prove a negative, so there's no work to do. You can't prove that there isn't an elephant inside the trunk of my car."[14]

It is true that you can't prove a negative. However, the existence of God is provable in the same way a building is positive proof that there was a builder. But the atheist is quick to respond that the "building, therefore a builder" analogy doesn't work, because a building is inanimate. It doesn't have life; therefore it needed a builder. Nature, they say, is organic—animals, insects, plants, fish, human beings, and so forth, have life, can reproduce, and therefore they don't necessitate a Creator. There is a small problem for that belief. You have to forget about mountains, the oceans, the clouds, the sun, the stars, and the entire *non*organic planet on which we live. What do atheists think those things are made of? All of them are nonorganic. The elephant of which Jillette spoke isn't inside the trunk. It's sitting on his knee, and he doesn't see him because of a solipsistic worldview, subtly disguised as open-mindedness.

Mr. Jillette continued, "So, anyone with a love for truth outside of herself has to start with no belief in God and then look for evidence of God. She needs to search for some objective evidence of a supernatural power. All the people I write e-mails to often are still stuck at this searching stage. The atheism part is easy." [15] With due respect, atheism is not easy in the slightest. It takes a huge amount of faith to be an atheist.

Most atheists bristle at the thought that atheism has anything to do with faith, but not Penn Jillette. Look at his faith: "But, this 'This I Believe' thing seems to demand something more personal, some leap of faith that helps one see life's big picture, some rules to live by. So, I'm saying, 'This I believe: I believe there is no God.'" And then from there he builds his entire life's philosophy:

> Having taken that step, it informs every moment of my life. I'm not greedy. I have love, blue skies, rainbows and Hallmark cards, and that has to be enough. It has to be enough, but it's everything in the world and everything in the world is plenty for me. It seems just rude to beg the invisible for more. Just the love of my family that raised me and the family I'm raising now is enough that I don't need heaven. I won the huge genetic lottery and I get joy every day. [16]

This is why atheism is difficult. Jillette believes that the entire universe—with its vast planets and their own orbits; suns and moons; the earth, spinning through space, with its oceans and daily tides; the yearly seasons; all the succulent fruits; the amazing animals, both male and female; the beautiful flowers; the marvels of the fearfully and wonderfully made human body, also with male and female, reproducing after its own kind; as well as millions of other marvels of nature—all happened because nothing created it. Such a belief takes huge faith. It denies all logic, reason, and common sense. It would be far easier to believe that there was nothing, and that nothing for no reason exploded into a fully loaded and flying jumbo jet, with passengers, pilots, and crew. If I could believe that for a moment, I would be a "fool." That's the word the Bible uses to describe the atheist (Psalm 14:1), and it further says, "Do not speak in the hearing of a fool, for he will despise the wisdom of your words" (Proverbs 23:9 NKJV).

James Cameron: For many years, film producer James Cameron was a closet atheist, hiding as an "agnostic" from the real world of atheism. The word *agnostic* comes from the Greek word *agnōstos*, which means "unknown, unknowable," and has grown to mean someone who doesn't know if God exists. An agnostic is like a man who looks at the finished production of a major motion picture and is sure if there was a producer. It may have been caused by an explosion in some studio a long time ago, or it may have had a producer, but he's not sure. Such a person would be better classified as "unthinking" than "not knowing." How could any movie make itself, without the involvement of an army of scriptwriters, graphic artists, actors, grips, sets, a production crew of sound and lighting experts, editors, and a million and one other things necessary for a major motion picture production? The agnostic lives in a fog of oblivion when it comes to God.

Eventually James Cameron didn't feel comfortable with just being an agnostic. He called it "cowardly atheism." One day he decided to take courage, and so he said, "I've sworn off agnosticism, which I now call cowardly atheism. I've come to the position that in the complete absence of any supporting data whatsoever for the persistence of the individual in some spiritual form, it is necessary to operate under the provisional conclusion that there is no afterlife and then be ready to amend that if I find out otherwise."[17]

James Cameron is no longer in doubt about the existence of God, because one day he took a leap of faith from agnosticism (not knowing if God exists) into the world of atheism (a disbelief in the existence of deity). The doubt went and conclusive faith came because of "a complete absence of any supporting data whatsoever." That led him to his "provisional" conclusion. He has made no provision for the existence of God, and he won't make any provision until he finds otherwise.

That sounds vaguely familiar. Designers of a large ship many years ago were so sure it couldn't sink that they made no provision for such a disaster. They had so much faith in themselves and their design of the ocean liner that they hardly gave the need for lifeboats a second thought. You would think that if anyone had learned a lesson from such pride-filled arrogance, it would be James Cameron, who directed the epic film about that very ship.

The overconfidence of the *Titanic* designers wasn't amendable. They couldn't fix the problem of the sinking ship *after* it struck the iceberg. It was too late; there was no second chance. When the passengers called for help, none came.

Imagine being on the Southampton dock back on April 10, 1912, knowing that five days later the unsinkable *Titanic* would sink like a rock. It would go to the bottom of the icy ocean, taking with it 1,502 precious human lives. If you had any foreknowledge of the disaster, what would you say to the passengers as they excitedly boarded the ship? You couldn't remain silent. Such is the plight of the Christian. We can't remain silent because we know what the future holds.

There is sure hope for those who humble themselves in this life, repent, and trust in Jesus alone, but once we sink into the icy waters of death, there's no second chance. If we die in our sins, we will get justice from a holy Creator, and there isn't a hope in hell. Jesus said, "Go into all the world and preach the gospel to every creature. He who believes and is baptized will be saved; but he who does not believe will be condemned" (Mark 16:15–16 NKJV). "Condemned" means just what it says, and "saved" means what it says.

Roger Ebert: As we have seen, atheists distance themselves from any talk of faith. They even go to great pains to define themselves as having "no belief" in any gods. Well-known movie critic Roger Ebert agreed. He once said, "Many readers have informed me that it is a tragic and dreary business to go into death without faith. I don't feel that way. 'Faith' is neutral."[18]

Just before he died of cancer in April 2013, he said this about his impending death: "I know it is coming, and I do not fear it, because I believe there is nothing on the other side of death to fear."[19] Faith and fear are opposites. If you are fearful of stepping into an elevator, it's because you lack faith in it. If you have faith and therefore trust it, you won't fear. Ebert didn't fear death because of what he "believed." Because he believed, he had *faith*; he *trusted* that there was nothing after death.

As a Christian, I trust that there is life after death. This is because my faith is in the Son of the living God—the One who forgave my sins and in an instant of time transformed my life. My trust is in Him who said, "I am the resurrection and the life. He who believes in Me, though he may die, he shall live. And whoever lives and believes in Me shall never die" (John 11:25–26 NKJV). But look at where Ebert placed his faith: "I am comforted by Richard Dawkins' theory of memes," he said. His faith in the words of Professor Richard Dawkins gave him comfort in his death. He placed his trust in the words of a man who believes that God "probably" doesn't exist, has no training in theology, thinks he's a talking primate, considers himself a distant cousin of the banana and the turnip, and believes that we could have been seeded by aliens.

If Jesus Christ was a liar and there is no afterlife, then Roger Ebert will never know it. Death is the end. But if the Son of God spoke the truth and there is a real hell (see Mark 9:47–48), then Ebert died deceived, and will have eternity to despise Dawkins for his lies and deception.

Jodie Foster, Hugh Hefner, and others: Jodie Foster once asked "How could you ask me to believe in God when there's absolutely no evidence that I can see?"[21] She also said, "People are always surprised when I say that I'm an atheist."[22] I am surprised that anyone can profess to be an atheist. Perhaps her "that I can see" is telling. Even Helen Keller, who was born blind and deaf, could "see" God. No doubt, in her silent darkness, every fragrant flower, every ray of the warm sun, every taste that touched her tongue told her that there was a God who created all things. Jodie Foster shouldn't therefore be surprised that people are surprised that she's an atheist.

Despite her atheism, though, she and her family do celebrate both Christmas and Hanukah. She has also stated that she has "great respect for all religions" and spends "a lot of time studying divine texts, whether it's Eastern religion or Western religion."[23]

In early 2013, when Jodie Foster took the stage to accept her Cecil B. DeMille Lifetime Achievement Award at the Golden Globes, "without explicitly stating that she was gay, the message was evident. 'I'm just going to put it out there, loud and proud . . . I am, uh, single,' she said."[24] I believe that many of us who are Christians have hesitated to clearly state where the Bible stands when it comes to homosexuality, perhaps for fear of being considered hateful. Allow me to try and explain why I think we have failed to communicate the hope of Christianity, particularly to the homosexual community.

Think for a moment of the many police officers who have a steady job because of thieves. If there were no thieves—no purse-snatchers, pickpockets, bank robbers, burglars, cybercrime, identity theft, Ponzi schemes, insider trading, bribery, money laundering, credit card theft, muggings, fraud, white-collar crime, etc., millions of law officers around the world would be out of a job. Even though theft is clearly bad for any society, some could put forth the argument that it is beneficial.

So it may not be wise, if I wanted to speak

against theft, to say that theft is bad for society. Instead, as a Christian, I would simply say that theft is morally wrong because God says it's wrong. Case closed. This is what God's Word says about the subject:

> Do you not know that the unrighteous will not inherit the kingdom of God? Do not be deceived. Neither fornicators, nor idolaters, nor adulterers, nor homosexuals, nor sodomites, nor *thieves*, nor covetous, nor drunkards, nor revilers, nor extortioners will inherit the kingdom of God. (1 Corinthians 6:9–10 NKJV, emphasis added)

Similarly, I would be unwise to say that homosexuality is bad for society. This is because if it can be shown that homosexuals make good pilots, good movie producers, good doctors and dentists, and good parents, they win the argument. Case closed.

But the real tragedy is that the dispute about the detrimental effects of homosexuality makes the cross of Jesus Christ irrelevant. If homosexuality isn't seen to be a sin, as the Bible clearly states that it is, then homosexuals won't see their need of a Savior. On top of that, the argument makes Christians seem like a hate group, because they don't want homosexuals to have equal rights.

If we say that homosexuality is wrong, we should do so because we want homosexuals to enter the kingdom of God. We should speak out loud and clear because we care about Jodie Foster and others, and where they spend eternity. We should also care about fornicators, idolaters, adulterers, thieves, the covetous, drunkards, revilers, and extortioners.

Each of these groups is in terrible danger, and they are not aware of it because they are not hearing the truth in love, from the Church. But if we don't warn them (as Penn Jillette once said), we are truly being hateful. And if we are hated for the truth, our consolation is that we are not giving an opinion. We are simply stating what the Scriptures say, and therefore anyone who disagrees has a disagreement with the Word of God, and not with the Church. We stand behind the biggest coattails in the universe.

Hugh Hefner said, "I believe in the creation, and therefore I believe there has to be a creator of some kind, and that is my God."[25] His god didn't mind pornography.

You will find Steve Jobs, the cofounder of Apple Inc., listed on "Celebrity Atheists."[26] However, he certainly wasn't an atheist. Just after his tragic death in October 2011, National Public Radio said, "Jobs told Isaacson that he was '50/50' on the existence of God, and that he wasn't sure whether there was an afterlife."[27]

In his last interview (with *Playboy* magazine), just before he was tragically murdered, John Lennon said:

I don't believe in the evolution of fish to monkeys to men. . . . It's absolutely irrational garbage. . . . They set up these idols and then they knock them down. It keeps all the old professors happy in the university. It gives them something to do. . . . Everything they told me as a kid has already been disproved by the same type of 'experts' who made them up in the first place."[28]

(To Professor Dawkins, John Lennon must have been "ignorant, stupid, insane, or wicked.")

I was once told by a high-profile atheist that Lennon's famous song "Imagine" was the atheist's anthem. But when John Lennon himself was asked about the song's meaning, he had this to say: "Dick Gregory gave Yoko and me a . . . prayer book. It is in the Christian idiom, but you can apply it anywhere. It is the concept of positive prayer. If you want to get a car, get the car keys? Get it? That's what "Imagine" is saying. If you can *imagine* a world at peace, with no denominations of religion—not without religion but without this my-God-is-bigger-than-your-God thing—then it can be true."[29] John Lennon wasn't a Christian, but he was certainly not an atheist.

Did you know that the famous song "Stand by Me" has been recorded by more than four hundred artists, or that John Lennon's YouTube version received more than 35 million views? If you know your Bible, the lyrics may sound a little familiar: "If the sky that we look upon should tumble and fall / and the mountains should crumble to the sea . . ." That's because the song was inspired, in part, by Psalm 46:2–3. It also got its inspiration from the spiritual "Lord Stand by Me." [30] Sadly, removing "Lord" and replacing it with "Darling, darling" doesn't make sense. When four bullets entered the back of John Lennon, Yoko Ono couldn't stand by him, because he was dead in minutes. He was gone.

No one can stand by you when you pass into eternity—except God, because He's the only one who transcends death. So if you're snatched into eternity today by an accident, you die by cancer, or you simply die in your sleep, you can have One who stands by you. I came into this world with nothing, but I leave with my hand in the hand of Jesus. I wouldn't swap that for a solid-gold 18-wheeler semitruck fully laden with precious diamonds.

Chapter 4
MORE FAMOUS ATHEISTS

Steven Salzberg wrote a condescending *Forbes* magazine article that ridiculed those who believe that God created the universe, maintaining that his articles are "celebrating good science by fighting pseudoscience and bad medicine." This "good science" article was called "Evolution bugs people" and was accompanied by a fascinating picture of three leaf insects. He wrote:

> The photo shows three "walking leaves," or leaf insects, which have evolved to look just like the leaves around them. These little bugs must be one of the best examples of natural selection ever. The more closely they resemble a leaf, the more difficult it is for predators to find them. Over the millenia, the bugs who evaded predators survived better, and eventually walking leaves looked like they do today.[1]

He then tells us why he believes these walking leaf insects are the best examples of natural selection:

> In fact, these guys have been around for a long time, at least 47 million years, according to a fossil discovery published in 2006. That paper described a fossilized leaf insect found in an ancient lake bed in Germany, which looks remarkably similar to its modern descendants.

Yet despite this amazing evidence, only 40% of Americans believe in evolution."[2]

Salzberg believes that the bugs have been around for "at least 47 million years" because he has unquestioning faith in the 2006 report of the fossil discovery. Those who discovered the fossil believed it was that old because they had faith in their own dating process. But Salzburg then said that the 47 million–year-old fossilized leaf insect "looks remarkably similar to its modern descendants." Let's think about this for a moment. It looks "remarkably similar" to a *modern bug*. In other words there was little or no difference between the old and the new bug. *The reason that there was no change after 47 million years of "evolution" is because it didn't evolve at all.* God made the leaf bug as it is—an amazing bug that can make itself look like a leaf. Salzburg's faulty conclusion isn't "celebrating good science." It's a blind faith in the fantasy of evolution.

This was on my Facebook page recently: "Bonobos are our closest DNA relatives. Why do the vast, vast majority of scientists accept it? Over 99% of relevant scientists do. Julie, you do not understand what a theory is if you say that." [Jim]

Be careful what you believe when it comes to what believers in evolution tell you. You have to always keep in mind that someone who has faith in evolution usually embraces atheism, which means that they have no moral compass. This means they can stretch the truth without any qualms of conscience—not that Jim is doing that here. More than likely he is just using the usual "tactics" he has learned from other believers. Let's look at three points made by him:

1. "Bonobos are our closest DNA relatives." Bonobos are pygmy chimpanzees, and the fact that they have DNA doesn't make them relatives. They also have skin, arms, legs, a brain, blood, eyes, kidneys, liver, lungs, etc., but the similarity to human beings doesn't mean that we are a branch of primates. It just means that God used a similar blueprint when He made both man and primates. But that blueprint isn't confined to those two parts of His creation. Pigs also have eyes, ears, heart, liver, lungs, kidneys, DNA, blood, hair, brains, etc. I sometimes sound like a pig when I sleep, know people that eat like pigs, and if we need a skin transplant surgeons will often use pigskin, because it's the closest to human skin. Does that mean we have a common ancestor in the pig? It could, if you are a believer in evolution— because there are no hard and fast rules.

2. "Why do the vast, vast majority of scientists accept it? Over 99% of relevant scientists do." Notice the word "relevant." In other words, anyone who doesn't believe in evolution is relegated to irrelevancy. They

are not counted. I could say that 100% of "relevant" scientists accept creationism, and be speaking the truth because I count those that don't accept it to be incompetent, and therefore I haven't included them in my statistic.

3. "Julie, you do not understand what a theory is if you say that." Believers in evolution can move the goalposts at any time. This means that if you have scored a point, they can say you haven't. They can redefine the theory at any time, because there are no definitive rules. But this is no game. It is more serious than a heart attack. Someone who believes the bogus claims of evolution, by default, reject the biblical account of creation and therefore the gospel of Jesus Christ. That will make them all-time losers, and that's a tragedy beyond words.[3]

Now let's return to the subject of famous atheists.

Jesse Ventura: Well-known atheist Jesse Ventura said, when speaking of the war in the Middle East: "Most every war that happens on this planet is due to the fact of religion. One religion doesn't like the way another religion worships God, 'so we're going to kill you.' I love religion, you know, and I say that sarcastically. . . . And I say that because—I've openly admitted I'm an atheist."[4]

Does he really think that the U.S. Civil War, which claimed 750,000 lives, was a religious war?

Does he believe that the First World War, which claimed 20 million lives, was a religious war? Does he think that the Second World War, which took 50 million lives, was a religious war? In the last one hundred or so years, there have been more than three hundred major wars. Most of them were political and had nothing to do with religion.

ARE ATHEISTS DISHONEST?

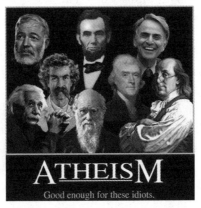

I don't believe that all atheists are dishonest. I have many atheist friends who do have some sense of integrity. But to fundamentalist believers in atheism, there's no such thing as absolute right or wrong. Lying is not a sin. For example, on a popular atheist poster (see poster, above) are pictures of Ernest Hemingway, Abraham Lincoln, Carl Sagan, Mark Twain, Thomas Jefferson, Benjamin Franklin, Albert Einstein, and Charles Darwin, along with the words: "Atheism—Good enough for these idiots."

But Abraham Lincoln was not an atheist. He said, "Sir, my concern is not whether God is on our side; my greatest concern is to be on God's side, for God is always right."[5]

Neither was Carl Sagan. In a March 1996 profile by Jim Dawson in the *Minneapolis Star-Tribune*, Sagan talked about his then-new book *The Demon Haunted World* and was asked about his personal spiritual views. He said, "An agnostic is somebody who doesn't believe in something until there is evidence for it, so I'm agnostic."

Mark Twain certainly wasn't an atheist. He said, among other things, "None of us can be as great as God, but any of us can be as good."[6]

Benjamin Franklin, another purported atheist, said, "The longer I live, the more convincing proofs I see of this truth, that God governs in the affairs of men. And if a sparrow cannot fall to the ground without His notice, is it probable that an empire can rise without His aid?"[7]

Thomas Jefferson wasn't an atheist. According to the *LA Times*, he said, "Say nothing of my religion. It is known to myself and my God alone. Its evidence before the world is to be sought in my life; if that has been honest and dutiful to society, the religion which has regulated it cannot be a bad one."[8]

See if you can guess the identity of these two famous atheists: the first was a minister of a large church when he converted to atheism, and the second atheist was a strong believer in evolution who became instantly famous around the globe back in 1994:

1. "Our people, I would say, are ninety percent atheist. . . . I felt somewhat hypocritical for the last years as I became an atheist. . . . My bishop knows that I'm an atheist. . . . He must have spent twenty thousand dollars traveling around, hoping to get my denomination to remove me, because I was so atheistic."

2. "If a person doesn't think there is a God to be accountable to, then what's the point of trying to modify your behavior to keep it within acceptable ranges? That's how I thought anyway. I always believed the theory of evolution as truth, that we all just came from the slime. When we died, you know, that was it, there is nothing."

Answers: The first atheist was the Reverend Jim Jones of Jonestown and Peoples Temple. He led 909 men, women, and children in mass suicide in 1978.[9] The second atheist and evolutionist was Jeffrey Dahmer, who murdered seventeen men and boys, dismembering them, storing their parts, and indulging in cannibalism and necrophilia.[10]

Of course, not all atheists are mass murderers. I have many atheist friends, and they are kind and loving people. However, if you are thinking of becoming an atheist, know this: atheism will leave you with no moral boundaries, except what you feel is right and what society says is morally okay. If the government says it's okay to kill babies in the womb, then it's okay. It's a human right. If society says adultery, homosexuality, fornication, lust, pornography, and lying are okay, then so be it.

If in ten years' time society says that pedophiles are born with a different orientation, and they therefore have their First Amendment right to do what they do in private, that's okay. The same rudderless standard applies to euthanasia, mass sterilization, genocide, bestiality, and necrophilia. If there are no moral absolutes, then clearly anything goes. It's simply a matter of consensus.

There is one really big problem though—"He has appointed a day on which He will judge the world in righteousness by the Man whom He has ordained" (Acts 17:31 NKJV). This isn't the old man in the sky reaching out to Adam. This is the omnipresent Creator who made this great earth, the massive sun, and the immense universe. He is morally perfect, wrath-filled at all evil, and He is to be greatly feared. Using personification, the Bible says that the whole of creation will rejoice on the Day of Judgment—because that's the day when justice will be done. Have you ever rejoiced when some devious, bloodthirsty, and cruel mass murderer was caught and brought to justice? That's what that means about creation rejoicing. Those who are evil will get exactly what they have coming to them . . . and that's good. That will be the day when murderers, rapists, thieves, liars, the covetous, adulterers, extortioners, fornicators, those who have hated, looked with lust, blasphemed, etc., will get perfect justice. Hell is God's prison—His place of punishment, and there will be no parole. However, God is rich in mercy and in His great kindness. He provided a means of forgiveness. He can let us live.

Chapter 5

EDISON, HITCHINS, GATES, EINSTEIN, AND OTHERS

Thomas Edison: You will find this famous inventor listed on Celebrity Atheists, on Positive Atheism, and on other atheist sites.[1] Despite their claims, Thomas Edison wasn't a doubting Thomas. Like many thinking minds, he simply hated the hypocrisy of "religion" and saw no evidence of an afterlife, but he was never an atheist. This is what he said:

> There is a great directing head of people and things—a Supreme Being who looks after the destinies of the world. I am convinced that the body is made up of entities that are intelligent and are directed by this Higher Power. When one cuts his finger, I believe it is the intelligence of these entities which heals the wound. When one is sick, it is the intelligence of these entities which brings convalescence. You know that there are living cells in the body so tiny that the microscope cannot find them at all. The entities that give life and soul to the human body are finer still and lie infinitely beyond the reach of our finest scientific instruments. When these entities leave the body, the body is like a ship without a rudder—deserted, motionless and dead.[2]

Henry Ford once said: "I believe God is managing affairs and that He doesn't need any advice from me. With God in charge, I believe everything will work out for the best in the end. So what is there to worry about?" Ford was a very close friend of Edison, and after his death, he said, "He felt there was a central processing core of life that went on and on. That was his conclusion. We talked of it many times together. . . . Call it religion or what you like, Mr. Edison believed that the universe was alive and that it was responsive to man's deep necessity. It was an intelligent and hopeful religion if there ever was one. Mr. Edison went away expecting light, not darkness."

Christopher Hitchens: Christopher Hitchens was likable, fascinating, intelligent, and extremely eloquent. He was also audacious, in that it seemed that he didn't care what people thought of him. Most of us care about how we comb our hair or what we wear, but it was as though Hitchens didn't care. (He may have been like a friend I once had many years ago, who made sure he looked as though he didn't care about his appearance. He spent a great deal of time looking into a mirror, making sure that his hair was a mess and his clothes were unkempt. His image was one of humility, but he was actually very conceited.)

Most human beings have enough sense to know that if they work in a city that has a serious smog problem, it's wise to either stay indoors or at least wear a mask that will filter out the poison. But cigarette smokers have their own little concentrated toxic smog pack that they don't avoid. They pay money to breathe in the poison in a concentrated form, and in the end they certainly pay for such recklessness. Each of us should think of the future. Every puff on a cigarette is another tick closer to a time bomb explosion of terrible consequences. Christopher Hitchens didn't care about the consequences of smoking cigarettes. Tragically, he died of throat cancer in December of 2011. He once said:

> One must state it plainly. Religion comes from the period of human prehistory where nobody—not even the mighty Democritus who concluded that all matter was made from atoms—had the smallest idea what was going on. It comes from the bawling and fearful infancy of our species, and is a babyish attempt to meet our inescapable demand for knowledge (as well as for comfort, reassurance and other infantile needs). Today the least educated of my children knows much more about the natural order than any of the founders of religion, and one would like to think—though the connection is not a fully demonstrable one—that this is why they seem so uninterested in sending fellow humans to hell.[3]

In two short sentences Hitchens concluded that no one in Bible times "had the smallest idea what was going on." God gave ignorant Moses the Ten Commandments that could be summed up in two commandments that, if kept, would mean that the millions of laws on the books of educated contemporary society could be deleted. Was Hitchens willfully ignorant of those two commandments that solve almost every one of humanity's problems? Did he ever condescend to study the wisdom of Solomon?

He boasted that the least educated of his children knew more about the "natural order," presumably a reference to the unobservable, unscientific, unproven natural order of atheistic evolution. Such talk makes me wonder if he even explained to his children the meaning of the terms "B.C." and "A.D."—or did he conclude that the life of Jesus of Nazareth was inconsequential? Was Jesus just another ignorant human being who didn't have the smallest idea what was going on?

I also wonder if his offspring are living as hard and fast as their father. I hope not. I hope they saw his life as a testimony of what happens when a person gives no thought to the future, and that they take care of their health and live long and happy lives. Most of all, I hope they have open minds and plans, not only for their future, but for eternity.

Bill Gates: It's well known in atheist circles that Microsoft's Bill Gates is an atheist. You will find the billionaire listed on "Celebrity Atheists" and on many other atheist sites.[4] He is even held up as proof that atheists are generous philanthropists.[5]

But in an article titled "Bill Gates interview: I have no use for money. This is God's work," in the *Telegraph*, Gates said, "[Terrorism is] not going to stop us succeeding. It does force us to sit down with the Pakistan government to renew their commitments, see what they're going to do in security and make changes to protect the women who are doing God's work and getting out to these children and delivering the vaccine."[6] Billionaire Bill Gates is not an atheist.

Albert Einstein: The faith of some of the more crusading fundamental atheists was no doubt bolstered by a letter written by Einstein,[7] in which he said, "The word god is for me nothing more than the expression and product of human weaknesses, the Bible a collection of honourable, but still primitive legends which are nevertheless pretty childish. No interpretation no matter how subtle can (for me) change this."[8]

It was heralded by some as evidence for a denial of the existence of God, but this letter is consistent with the beliefs Einstein held throughout his life. He had previously stated, "I have repeatedly said that in my opinion the idea of a personal God is a childlike one."[9] He refused to put a personal name to the Creator. To Einstein, He wasn't the "I AM" of the Jews, or the "Jesus" of the Christians. The Creator was impersonal and unknowable. The word *God* was childlike and an expression and product of human weakness that fell short of Einstein's "idea" of the Creator, but he was never an atheist. He was even angered by those who alleged that he was, saying, "In view of such harmony in the cosmos which I, with my limited human understanding, am able to recognize, there are yet people who say there is no God. But what really makes me angry is that they quote me for the support of such views."[10]

In his book *The God Delusion*, atheist Richard Dawkins does precisely what angered Einstein in saying that he was an atheist.[11] Yet when asked if he had a belief in God, Einstein clearly replied, "I am not an atheist."[12] He even said, "The fanatical atheists are like slaves who are still feeling the weight of their chains which they have thrown off after hard struggle. They are creatures who—in their grudge against traditional religion as the 'opium of the masses'—cannot hear the music of the spheres."[13] Despite this, fanatical atheists still claim him as one of their own. An undeterred Richard Dawkins said, "Along with various other sources, this letter finally confirms that Einstein was, in every realistic sense of the word, an atheist."[14]

But he wasn't. And neither was Charles Darwin. He referred to God seven times in *Origin of Species*. He also said, "In my most extreme fluctuations I have never been an Atheist in the sense of denying the existence of a God. I think that generally (and more and more as I grow older), but not always, that an Agnostic would be a more correct description of my state of mind."[15]

So, out of the eight famous men on the poster, there is only one who was an atheist—Ernest Hemingway. And according to his biographer, back in 1961 Hemingway "pushed two shells into the twelve-gauge Boss shotgun, put the end of the barrel into his mouth, pulled the trigger and blew out his brains."[16]

There's your poster boy for atheism.

Chapter 6

THE GOOD DELUSION

In 2012, Richard Dawkins released a television series in which he asked the question, "If there is no God watching us, why be good?" He also examined the argument that "religion's absolutist moral codes fuel lies and guilt." It was a three-part series, titled "Sex, Death and the Meaning of Life" and explored "what happens if we leave religion behind." He also asked the question, "Can science bring understanding in the face of death, help us tell right from wrong, or reveal the meaning of life?" The first episode began with the professor declaring, "More and more of us realize there is no god, and yet religion still has a hold over us. I think ideas of saints and sinners, heaven and hell, still shape our thinking. I want to give you a scientific alternative. This series is not about whether God exists or not. It explores more challenging questions."[1]

The "fact" that God doesn't exist isn't challenging. All you have to do is believe the scientific impossibility that nothing created everything, and move on. Or you could do the unthinkable and redefine "nothing" as something, but still call it "nothing." The more challenging question in Dawkins's mind is, "What will guide and inspire us in a world without gods?"

The answer to the question, "If there is no

God, can we still be good?" is "Of course we can." We need only define our own meaning of the word "good." Is a rapist good if he boasts that he hasn't raped a woman for some time? Was Hitler good for Germany because he righted their economy and brought in full employment? Is a prostitute good for men who are looking for pleasure?

Dictionary.com gives forty-one definitions of "good" as an adjective. But that may not be as *good* as it seems because it adds to the confusion. Number one on the *good* list is the definition "morally excellent; virtuous; righteous; pious: a good man."[2] Then the page goes on to tell us that it can also mean "satisfactory in quality, quantity, or degree: a good teacher; good health." This same adjective, "good," can be used to describe a well-behaved child, a sound education, an untarnished name, or a philanthropic deed. You can have good credit. Fruit can be good for you; you can get good advice, or receive good news. You can have a good time, have a good figure, have good friends, and you can catch a good supply of food after a good day of fishing. You can have good manners, good weather, good soil, and you can enjoy a good ride on the good ship *Lollipop*.

So the dictionary gives the good professor lots of wiggle room in his thought that he can be good without God. In his program he says, "I'm going to explore the power the religious idea of sin has over our lives, explain why it's unhelpful and show

how we cause reason and science to find a better way to be good."

To Professor Richard Dawkins "good" is what he says it is. He is a law unto himself. The higher Law that says, "You shall not commit adultery, you shall not lie, kill, or steal" is unhelpful. Science has a better way. But the professor's science law doesn't get rid of God's Law. It is eternal, ever-presiding, and it will judge the whole of humanity by its perfect standard. The Law is like a mirror. It simply reflects what we are morally. It shows us that we are unclean so that we will go to the Savior to be cleansed of the filth of sin.

The same dictionary says that "sin" is "transgression of divine law."[3] It isn't the existence of God that offends the atheist. It's the moral demands that come from God that cause the animosity. Look at how Scripture explains this: "Because the carnal mind is enmity against God: for it is not subject to the law of God, neither indeed can be" (Romans 8:7 NKJV).

Professor Dawkins's godless (carnal) mind is deeply offended by God and His Law for the same reason a criminal is antagonistic toward criminal law. The lawbreaker hates the police because they stand for that which is right, good, and just.

If you feel the same as the professor and you have a problem with Christianity, please put aside that offense and think instead of your bigger problem. Death for you isn't just an elephant in the room. It's much bigger than that. It has its massive foot on your head, and it's just a matter of time until it lets its full weight come down.

I love the scene in the movie *Ben Hur* where a Roman soldier is marching condemned galley slaves through the desert. They stop in Nazareth for a break, but as the thirsty slaves are being given water, the head honcho says that Judah Ben Hur wasn't to have a drop. Judah collapses on the ground and gasps, "God help me!" Suddenly, a shadow comes over him and a hand gently lifts his weary head from the dirt and pours water between his parched lips. I have watched that scene numerous times and have never failed to sob like a child, because what I see is so similar to what happened to me in my conversion experience.

At the age of twenty, I began to think deeply about life. I was very successful, financially secure, extremely happy, healthy, I was my own boss, had a loving and beautiful wife . . . and I was suddenly very aware that despite all my happiness, I was waiting around to die. It seemed that the whole of humanity was in a long line, moving closer and closer to a one-thousand-foot cliff, and were, one by one, jumping off to their deaths. It was as though everyone accepted the inevitability of it; no one was trying to get out of line. So I, ever so reluctantly, stood in line and waited for my turn.

At age twenty-two I heard the gospel for the first time. I am not exaggerating in saying that I was like Ben Hur, lying hopelessly in the dirt, and Jesus turned my head and poured the waters of life between my parched lips. I cannot express the relief and joy I found when I received the gift of everlasting life. To try and explain it to a non-Christian is like trying to explain light to a man who has been born blind. To use another somewhat lacking analogy, it's like looking at a crying, newly delivered baby. You know what he is crying for, so you put him on the mother's breast, and he immediately stops crying. He is suddenly gratified. He was born with an instinct to suckle, but he had no idea what he was looking for because he had never experienced it before.

I had no idea that in my darkness I was searching for light, until I found it in Jesus Christ (see John 8:31–32). He is the one who said "I am the light of the world. He who follows Me shall not walk in darkness, but have the light of life" (John 8:12 NKJV). And Jesus is the only one who can say, "Whoever drinks the water I give him will never thirst. Indeed, the water I give him will become in him a spring of water welling up to eternal life" (John 4:13 NIV).

Let's look at the word *good* once again. The first dictionary meaning was "moral excellence." The Bible's definition of "good" is moral perfection (see Matthew 5:48), and it tells us that the only God is good (Mark 10:17–18). From the standpoint of His moral perfection, none of us is good.

I do most of my writing from my home office. To my left is a large window that lets in the early morning sun. Before I raise the blind each morning, my desk looks perfectly clean. But as the very low-lying sun streams in from the east, it reveals—no matter how thoroughly I have dusted—tens of thousands of tiny dust particles. They are on my keyboard, down between the keys, on my screen, and all over the wood of the desk.

Let me pull up the blind for a moment and let the light of God's Law shine upon your heart. If you stay away from the light, like the professor, you will be deluded about your moral condition. So please allow me to do this. It may not be a pleasant experience, but it is a most necessary one.

Have you ever lied? Simply answer the question, yes or no. Have you stolen anything in your life—irrespective of its value? Yes or no? Have you ever used God's name in vain, even once? Have you ever looked with lust or hated anyone or been angry with someone without a just cause? The Bible says:

> You have heard that it was said to those of old, "You shall not commit adultery." But I say to you that whoever looks at a woman to lust for her has already committed adultery with her in her heart. (Matthew 5:27–28 NKJV)
>
> You have heard that it was said to those of old, "You shall not murder, and whoever murders will be in danger of the judgment."

But I say to you that whoever is angry with his brother without a cause shall be in danger of the judgment. (Matthew 5:21–22 NKJV)

If you have done these things, then you are a self-admitted lying thief, a blasphemer, a murderer, and an adulterer at heart. So what do you have to say for yourself? How can you justify murder of the heart, adultery, lying, stealing, and using God's name as a cuss word? Confessing your sins can't help you. That is like standing before a judge and confessing that you are guilty as charged. How can that help? Saying you are sorry and that you won't do it again won't help either. Of course a guilty criminal should be sorry, and of course he shouldn't commit the crimes again. So what can you do to make things right? How can you avoid being guilty on Judgment Day and being justly damned to hell?

We'll answer that question momentarily, but first, know this: every one of us has more than one "skeleton in the closet." It's more like a massive graveyard. Jeremiah 17:1 says, "The sin of Judah is written with a pen of iron, and with the point of a diamond: it is graven upon the table of their heart." We, like Judah, need only to check the tables of our own hearts to know the truth of this. A certain food smell or a few bars of an old tune can bring instant recall of a decadent event that took place in our lives many years ago. The conscious mind may have pushed the sinful things we have done aside temporarily, but every sin we have ever committed is locked up in a vault of the memory banks. It will be unlocked on the Day of Judgment and be evidence that will damn those who are found in their sins. I'm horrified at the thought of that happening to you.

Everything of which we should be ashamed— every immoral deed, every unclean thought, every lie, blasphemy, idle word, theft, or act of fornication—every transgression against that perfect Law is written on the tablet of the heart, and is waiting, "kept in store" for that Day (Romans 2:5–7). Please, don't die in your sins. Let the voice of your conscience expose them. Bring them to the light. All of us have seriously sinned against our Creator; we are under His terrible wrath, and the Bible says that there is nothing we can do to save ourselves.

What hope do we have, then? Keep reading.

RAVING LUNATICS

A woman's car broke down late one moonless night in an unfamiliar area. She was afraid, so she rolled the vehicle's windows up tight, locked the doors, and turned on the radio to keep herself company. She decided that it would be wise to wait until the morning light before going for help.

A short time later a frantic man appeared at her window and began to yell at her. Frightened, she gestured for him to go away. He left and then returned seconds later with a rock in his hand, smashed the window of her car, and pulled her out, much to the woman's horrified protests.

As they fell to the ground, several feet away, a massive train suddenly slammed into her car, causing it to burst into flames.

The man she thought was a raving lunatic was only trying to warn her.

You may consider Christians to be raving lunatics, but all we are frantically trying to do is warn you that you are in terrible danger. The train of God's moral Law will be merciless, and your ignorance of the imminent peril doesn't make it disappear.

But the Bible tells us that God is "rich in mercy" (Ephesians 2:4). Jesus portrayed Him as a loving father who is looking out for the return of his prodigal son. When he sees the boy at a distance, he runs to him, falls upon him, and kisses him (Luke 15:11–32). You are the prodigal, and God is that father. Think of what He did to save guilty sinners from damnation in hell—He sent His Son to Earth, and Jesus became a human being to pay our fine, so we could leave the courtroom. That's what took place on that terrible cross two thousand years ago. The sin of the world fell upon the innocent Lamb of God—He was bruised for *our* iniquities. The sweetest words that any human being will ever hear will be the words "Not guilty." God can wipe the desk perfectly clean in a moment of time because of the cross. The Bible says, "For God so loved the world, that he gave his only begotten Son, that whosoever believeth in him should not perish, but have everlasting life" (John 3:16).

Let me give you a special, "expanded" skeptic's version of John 3:16: "For God so loved the world that He gave His only begotten Son, that whoever believes in Him (has an unwavering confidence in Him that is similar to the confidence atheists and evolutionists have in dating methods, professors, and theories) shall not perish but have everlasting life (live forever on an incredible new earth—having pleasure forevermore, in a new body incapable of pain, suffering or death)."

Please surrender to God, and do it now, because you may not have tomorrow. Confess your sins to Him *and* with His help turn from them, and place your trust in Jesus Christ alone. If you are not sure what to say, pray a prayer similar to the one king David prayed (it is basically a sincere apology to God). He had committed adultery and murder, but after his sin was exposed, he cried:

> Have mercy upon me, O God, according to Your lovingkindness; according to the multitude of Your tender mercies, blot out my transgressions. Wash me thoroughly from my iniquity, and cleanse me from my sin. For I acknowledge my transgressions, and my sin is always before me. Against You,

You only, have I sinned, and done this evil in Your sight—that You may be found just when You speak, and blameless when You judge. Behold, I was brought forth in iniquity, and in sin my mother conceived me. Behold, You desire truth in the inward parts, and in the hidden part You will make me to know wisdom. Purge me with hyssop, and I shall be clean; wash me, and I shall be whiter than snow. Make me hear joy and gladness, that the bones You have broken may rejoice. Hide Your face from my sins, and blot out all my iniquities. Create in me a clean heart, O God, and renew a steadfast spirit within me. (Psalm 51:1–10)

Chapter 7
THE HORNET'S NEST

Paul Zachary ("PZ") Meyers is a biologist and associate professor at the University of Minnesota–Morris. He is also a popular atheist writer who has revealed a longstanding embarrassment about atheists who say that they "lack a belief in gods." In an attempt to try to legitimize the philosophy of atheism, he has distanced himself from those who misrepresent his personal convictions. But in his effort to swat those who bug him, he hit a hornet's nest. The reaction was stinging:

> Only this time it isn't a mob of religious fanatics and anti-choicers who have called me pond scum who will go to hell, an insect souled vile man, a black-souled amoral monster, pure evil, morally depraved, with a depraved mind, descend[ing] down the various stages into madness, and so forth," he said. "but I have this time managed to antagonize a bunch of *atheists*."[1]

And no wonder. He made the mistake of pointing out the nonexistent foundations of atheism. He showed how unthinking it is to say that you have "no beliefs in any gods." Modern atheists changed the definition of "atheist" from "someone who doesn't believe in the existence of

God," and in doing so, thought they had outwitted the opposition. They pled ignorance to the God issue. They believed that it was intelligent, but their "reasoning" wasn't clever. It was stupid, and the learned professor said so.

He who says he has no belief that there are any gods, *believes* that there is no evidence that any gods exist. Belief (trust) is the foundation for so many things in life—for marriage, for our convictions about history, for all human relationships, for the health of our monetary system, for flying in planes, for driving in cars, for eating food prepared in restaurants, for drinking bottled water, for taking medicine, for our convictions about the age of the earth, for calling a number on your phone, for having surgery, for accepting the hypothesis of evolution, and a million and one other things of which we have convictions.

In reference to the many atheists who believe that they *don't* have faith, Meyers betrayed their trust when he said:

> Boy, I really do hate these guys. You've got a discussion going, talking about why you're an atheist, or what atheism should mean to the community, or some such topic that is dealing with our ideas and society, and some smug [obscenity] comes along and announces that "Atheism means you lack a belief in gods. Nothing more. Quit trying to add meaning

to the term." As if atheism can only be some platonic ideal floating in virtual space with no connections to anything else; as if atheists are people who have attained a zen-like ideal, their minds a void, containing nothing but atheism, which itself is nothing. Dumbasses.[2]

But the professor didn't stop there. He also dismantled another foundational argument of modern atheism. One of their biggies is to say that we are all "born" atheists. As babes, we arrived on this earth with no belief in the existence of God. Meyers said of such infantile beliefs:

> Nope. Uh-uh. Same problem as the Dictionary Atheist—it implies atheism is simply an intellectual vacuum. Babies aren't Christians or Muslims or Hindus, and they aren't atheists, either, because we expect at least a token amount of thought is given to the subject. If babies are atheists, then so are trees and rocks—which is true by the dictionary definition, but also illustrates how ridiculously useless that definition is.

> Babies might also have an in-built predisposition to accept the existence of caring intelligences greater than themselves, so they might all lean towards generic theism, anyway. Mommy is God, after all.[3]

Next he took a swing at atheists who admit that they don't know for sure that God doesn't exist. He said:

> I have heard this so often, the hair-splitting grammatical distinctions some atheists think so seriously important in defining themselves. All you're doing is defining yourselves as [obscenity] retentive freaks, people! Get over it. Either way, you're an atheist—and that goes for the over-philosophized fussbudgets who insist that they're agnostics, not atheists, because they aren't 100% positive there aren't any gods, only 99 44/100ths positive.[4]

But this is the belief of the pope of atheism, Richard Dawkins. He said that he couldn't know for sure that there was no God. He told actor and political commentator Ben Stein that he was 99 percent sure God did not exist.[5] Professor Dawkins said:

> Well, technically, you cannot be any more than an agnostic. But I am as agnostic about God as I am about fairies and the Flying Spaghetti Monster. You cannot actually disprove the existence of God. Therefore, to be a positive atheist is not technically possible. But you can be as atheist about God as you can be atheist about Thor or Apollo. Everybody nowadays is an atheist about Thor and Apollo. Some of us just go one god further.[6]

No wonder angry bees came at Meyers from all angles. He even spoke to the nasty prejudice atheists had toward people of faith, lumping them in with murdering terrorists:

> Science flies you to the moon. Religion flies you into buildings. The second sentence is false. Religion does not turn you into a terrorist. The overwhelming majority of religious people have similar values to yours; my church-going grandmother would have been just as horrified at people using their faith to justify murdering people as the most hardened atheist, and there have been atheist individuals who also think they are justified in killing people for the cause. So stop saying this![7]

Good advice, professor. Those who love God don't hate anyone. They love atheists, and they even love their enemies. But the professor then tried to build up what he had just smashed down. He said:

> You are an atheist—take pride in what you do believe, not what you deny. And also learn to appreciate that the opposition hasn't arrived at their conclusions in a vacuum. There are actually deeper reasons that they so fervently endorse supernatural authorities, and they aren't always accounted for by stupidity.[8]

Yes, take pride in your scientifically impossible belief that nothing created everything, that you are nothing but a primate, and that you have no purpose for existence. Atheism leaves you with no knowledge of your origins, no understanding of what you are doing here on earth, and tells you nothing about what happens to you after you die. It gives you nothing of substance because it is nothing. It keeps you from repentance and faith in Jesus that will put the truth into your hands and bring everlasting life.

In spite of his spiritual blindness, I have to say that I like Professor Meyers. We have clashed many times over the years. I consider it a love/hate relationship—I love him, and he hates me. We of course disagree on the subjects of atheism and evolution, but I still respect him, because he isn't afraid to speak his mind.

AGREEING TO DISAGREE: A CONVERSATION

Early in 2009, I shared the gospel with a likable man named Jurgen Ankenbrand. I filmed the interesting encounter, and had it transcribed for this book:

RAY: Jurgen, are you a spiritual person?

JURGEN: No, I'm not.

RAY: Are you an atheist?

JURGEN: Yes, I am.

RAY: Do you know what the Golden Rule is?

JURGEN: Of what?

RAY: The Golden Rule.

JURGEN: No I—I don't know. Why don't you explain it to me?

RAY: You've never heard of it? "You shall love your neighbor as yourself."

JURGEN: Well, I love some of my neighbors and some I don't.

RAY: Some people you don't like?

JURGEN: True.

RAY: Now, why are you an atheist?

JURGEN: Because I don't believe in God.

RAY: So you believe nothing created everything?

JURGEN: I believe in the evolution theory.

RAY: So what created everything in the beginning?

JURGEN: Well, I wasn't there, so I don't have the details.

RAY: So you don't know what created everything?

JURGEN: No.

RAY: But obviously it wasn't nothing because nothing can't create anything, so something created everything in the beginning.

JURGEN: Maybe.

RAY: So you're not an atheist? You believe something created everything?

JURGEN: Yes, but I don't lose any sleep thinking about who and what might have done that.

RAY: Well, you should.

JURGEN: Why?

RAY: Because you've offended Him by sinning against His Law.

JURGEN: No . . .

RAY: Are you a good person, Jurgen?

JURGEN: I've heard you a lot of times [and] I've done the things you ask other people.

RAY: So you've lied and stolen?

JURGEN: So has everybody else under the sun.

RAY: Yes, but you're not going to answer for everyone on Judgment Day. You're going to have to answer for yourself, Jurgen. Are you going to be guilty or innocent on Judgment Day? I mean, have you looked at a woman and lusted for her?

JURGEN: When is Judgment Day?

RAY: Well, it's coming.

JURGEN: When?

RAY: Sure as hell, it's coming. God knows when it's coming.

JURGEN: What do you mean? You're referring to when you die . . . because as far as I'm concerned, when I'm physically dead, I'm dead and that's the end of it.

RAY: What if you're wrong?

JURGEN: Then so be it. Why should I concern myself with it now?

RAY: Do you care about your life?

JURGEN: Yes.

RAY: You love living?

JURGEN: Yes, of course.

RAY: Jurgen, Jesus said, "What shall it profit a man if he gains the whole world and loses his own soul?" He said, "If you look at a woman and lust for her, you've committed adultery with her in your heart." Have you ever looked at a woman with lust?

JURGEN: I'm sure every man has at one time or another.

RAY: Yes, but have you?

JURGEN: Yes.

RAY: Have you used God's name in vain?

JURGEN: Yes.

RAY: Even though you don't believe in Him?

JURGEN: I think it's more a matter of speech.

RAY: Yes. So I don't want you to end up in hell. You seem like a nice guy. I'd hate God to give you what you deserve on Judgment Day. You're a lying thief, a blasphemer, and an adulterer at heart.

JURGEN: Whatever will happen will happen. Like they say, "Que sera, sera."

RAY: Yeah, but that's a song.

JURGEN: Huh?

RAY: That's Hollywood. You don't want to put your faith in Hollywood and in love songs. . . . You want to put your faith in the Savior because He can wash away your sins so you're clean on Judgment Day, so God can let you live forever.

JURGEN: Why would I? Who wants to live forever?

RAY: I do.

JURGEN: I don't have enough money to live forever.

RAY: How old are you, Jurgen?

JURGEN: Sixty-eight.

RAY: How long have you got to live?

JURGEN: Probably another twenty years.

RAY: Are you afraid of dying?

JURGEN: No, not at all. If somebody were to tell me, "You're going to die next month," I'd say, "Okay, I've lived a full life and I have very few regrets, so I'm ready to go."

RAY: So you wouldn't have any treatment if you found you had cancer? You'd just yield to it? Say, "So what"?

JURGEN: I just had a triple bypass.

RAY: Why did you have a triple bypass?

JURGEN: Because I had a breathing problem. I used to jog here up and down, and all of a sudden one day, I had a hard time breathing, and so I went to hospital and they said, "You have a clogged arteries."

RAY: But hang on; you said that you don't mind dying. You should have just put up with it and died.

JURGEN: Yes, but it wasn't severe enough. It wasn't like I had cancer and you're going to die in a few weeks.

RAY: Yes, but . . . you let some person you don't know cut into your chest so you could live longer.

JURGEN: Why, you know why? Because it prevented me from living my life the way I want to live it. The way I lived the last forty years . . . running and being physically active and everything.

RAY: So, are you thankful for a healthy life?

JURGEN: Yes.

RAY: Who to?

JURGEN: (Silence) I contribute to having a healthy life by being active, by being physically fit.

RAY: Yes, but who are you grateful to for life? God gave you life!

JURGEN: Maybe so. But you can't prove your point any more than I can.

RAY: Yes, I can.

JURGEN: No.

RAY: Hang on. You can't say I can't, because I can.

JURGEN: Prove it.

RAY: All you have to do is do what the Bible says, repent and trust in Him who died on the cross for you. If you'll do that, if you'll repent and trust in the Savior . . . say, "God forgive my sins," and willfully put your trust in Jesus Christ, God will reveal Himself to you. This is what Jesus said, "He that has my commandments and keeps them, he it is that loves me and he that loves me will be loved by my Father. I, too, will love him and will reveal myself to him." So, there's the gauntlet. If you obey the gospel, God will reveal Himself to you.

JURGEN: I don't feel compelled to do any of the things you just said.

RAY: No? Well, let me leave the "ball in your court." Maybe tonight, you have a little, kind of minor heart attack on your bed, and you'll think about the issues of life and death and you'll say, "I'd better get right with God before death seizes upon me," because this is so important. Remember, Jesus said, "What shall it profit a man—"

JURGEN: Maybe to you it is, but to me it is not.

RAY: "—if he gains the whole world and loses his own soul?" Hey Jurgen, thank you so much for talking to me. I really appreciate it.

JURGEN: You're welcome. Have a good day!

December 23, 2010:

HUNTINGTON BEACH—A 69-year-old man riding his bicycle was killed after he was struck by two vehicles Wednesday, police said. Jurgen Ankenbrand, of Huntington Beach, was pronounced dead at about 5:40 P.M. at the scene of the crash, police said.[9]

Chapter 8

THE "SCIENCE" GUY

Back in September 2012, CBS News reported that Bill Nye had said, "Creationism is not appropriate for children." He added:

> You can believe what you want religiously. Religion is one thing, but science, provable science is something else. My concern is you don't want people growing up not believing in radioactivity, not believing in geology and deep time. You don't want people in the United States growing up without the expectation that we can land spacecraft on Mars. You want people to believe in science, this process, this great idea that humans had to discover more about the universe and our place in it, our place in space. And I really want to emphasize, I'm not attacking anybody's religion, but science, if you go to a museum and you see fossil dinosaur bones, they came from somewhere, and we have by diligent investigation determined that the earth is 4.54 billion years old.[1]

Notice his intermingling of the words "believe" and "know." He doesn't *know* that the earth is 4.54 billion years old. Rather, he is convinced it is that old, because he trusts those diligent folks who gave him the information. When asked why he is so passionate about his personal belief in evolution, Nye said:

> It's for the betterment of the United States, the United States economy and our future. What makes the United States great, the reason people wanted to live in the United States, move here still, is because of our ability to innovate. This goes back to Ben Franklin and Thomas Alva Edison and George Washington Carver, let alone landing on the moon, Neil Armstrong. All these people believed in science. This morning, talking about Hurricane Isaac, and we're watching satellite maps made with spacecraft orbiting the earth, and this all comes from science. If you have this idea that the earth is only 6,000 years old, you are denying, if you will, everything that you can touch and see. You're not paying attention to what's happening in the universe around you. As I say, this is bad for kids.[2]

His contention is that those who believe that God created the earth are antiscience. But there are a few things that Mr. Nye is not telling us when it comes to his name-dropping. Benjamin Franklin did believe in science, but he also believed in God. He said:

> I have lived, Sir, a long time, and the longer I live, the more convincing proofs I see

of this truth—*that God governs in the affairs of men.* And if a sparrow cannot fall to the ground with[out] his notice, is it probable that an empire can rise without his aid?[3]

George Washington Carver, the "father of modern agriculture" was a believer in science. But he also said, "Never since have I been without this consciousness of the Creator speaking to me. . . . The out of doors has been to me more and more a great cathedral in which God could be continuously spoken to and heard from."[4]

Astronaut Neil Armstrong believed in science and in God, and so did his fellow astronaut, Buzz Aldrin. Aldrin even celebrated communion on the moon, quoting the words of Jesus as he did so. Upon landing, he made the following announcement to Mission Control:

Houston, this is Eagle. . . . This is the LM pilot speaking. I would like to request a few moments of silence. I would like to invite each person listening in, whoever or wherever he may be, to contemplate for a moment the events of the last few hours, and to give thanks in his own individual way.[5]

He later related:

In the radio blackout, I opened the little plastic packages which contained the bread and the wine. I poured the wine into the chalice our church had given me. In the one-sixth gravity of the moon, the wine slowly curled and gracefully came up the side of the cup. Then I read the Scripture, "I am the vine, you are the branches. Whosoever abides in me will bring forth much fruit."

I had intended to read my communion passage back to earth, but at the last minute Deke Slayton had requested that I not do this. NASA was already embroiled in a legal battle with Madalyn Murray O'Hair, the celebrated opponent of religion, over the Apollo 8 crew reading from Genesis while orbiting the moon at Christmas. I agreed reluctantly.[6]

He then read Psalm 8:3–4: "When I consider thy heavens, the work of thy fingers, the moon and the stars, which thou hast ordained, what is man that thou art mindful of him? And the son of man, that thou visitest him?"

Again, Neil Armstrong did believe in science, but he was also a passionate believer in the Genesis account of creation. On December 24, 1968, in what was the most watched television broadcast at the time, the crew of Apollo 8 read in turn from the book of Genesis as they orbited the moon. Bill Anders, Jim Lovell, and Frank Borman recited verses 1 through 10 of chapter 1:

> Bill Anders: We are now approaching lunar sunrise and, for all the people back on Earth,

the crew of Apollo 8 has a message that we would like to send to you. "In the beginning God created the heavens and the earth. And the earth was without form, and void; and darkness was upon the face of the deep. And the Spirit of God moved upon the face of the waters. And God said, Let there be light: and there was light. And God saw the light, that it was good: and God divided the light from the darkness."

Jim Lovell: "And God called the light Day, and the darkness he called Night. And the evening and the morning were the first day. And God said, Let there be a firmament in the midst of the waters, and let it divide the waters from the waters. And God made the firmament, and divided the waters which were under the firmament from the waters which were above the firmament: and it was so. And God called the firmament Heaven. And the evening and the morning were the second day."

Frank Borman: "And God said, Let the waters under the heavens be gathered together unto one place, and let the dry land appear: and it was so. And God called the dry land earth; and the gathering together of the waters He called seas: and God saw that it was good." And from the crew of Apollo 8, we close with good night, good luck, a merry Christmas—and God bless all of you, all of you on the good earth."[7]

To insinuate that any of these men believed the Genesis account of creation is bogus, is disingenuous. Madalyn Murray O'Hair, the founder of American Atheists, Inc., tried to sue the United States government for the reading of Genesis in space, alleging a violation of the First Amendment. The lawsuit was dismissed by the Supreme Court, citing a lack of jurisdiction (the violation wasn't committed on Earth). O'Hair was tragically (and horribly) murdered some time later by a fellow atheist.[8]

Chapter 9

CAN THE BIBLE BE TRUSTED?

It's sadly evident that Richard Dawkins doesn't even know the very basics of the teachings of biblical Christianity. "Do you really mean to tell me the only reason you try to be good is to gain God's approval and reward, or to avoid his disapproval and punishment?" he asked.[1]

But the foundational teaching of the New Testament is that no one can attain God's approval or can gain a reward by being "good." There is no one who is good. Not one:

> The fool has said in his heart, "There is no God." They are corrupt, they have done abominable works, there is none who does good. The Lord looks down from heaven upon the children of men, to see if there are any who understand, who seek God. They have all turned aside, they have together become corrupt; there is none who does good, no, not one. (Psalm 14:1–3 NKJV)

The basis of our acceptance with God is something called "grace" (giving us what we don't deserve) through the medium of trust. We are told, "For by grace are you saved through faith, and that not of yourselves; it is the gift of God, not of works, lest anyone should boast" (Ephesians 2:8–9

NKJV). The reason any person has everlasting life is only because God is rich in mercy. Mercy is not giving us what we do deserve. We deserve hell, but God offers us heaven. The Judge has dismissed the case because the fine was paid by Another. This is what Christians call the sweet sound of an "amazing grace."

It's also evident that the professor doesn't know much about the Bible and what it teaches. He said:

> To be fair, much of the Bible is not systematically evil but just plain weird, as you would expect of a chaotically cobbled-together anthology of disjointed documents, composed, revised, translated, distorted and 'improved' by hundreds of anonymous authors, editors and copyists, unknown to us and mostly unknown to each other, spanning nine centuries.[2]

I have been reading the Bible every day without fail for more than forty years, and after diligent study, I can testify that it is not at all chaotic. It was written by *forty* different authors over fifteen hundred years, and it has one wonderful thread of continuity. In the Old Testament, God promised that He would deliver man from his greatest enemy—death, and in the New Testament we are told how He did that. There's no confusion. If I don't understand something, I can check the original wording in the Hebrew or Greek languages on my computer. Nothing has changed from when God's Word was written. There's been no random evolution when it comes to the Scriptures. God inspired the writers and He has preserved His Word.

The reason I believe the Bible is the Word of the Creator is because I have evidence that convinced me of that fact. It didn't convert me. It amazingly explained what had happened to me after my conversion. It also contains explicit and inexplicable prophecies that pinpoint humanity's timeline. The Scriptures warned that at the end of this age (not the end of the world), just before the second coming of Jesus, certain things would be happening:

1. There would be money-hungry Bible teachers, who would slur the Christian faith and deceive many: "There will be false teachers among you . . . and many will follow their destructive ways, because of whom the way of truth will be blasphemed. By covetousness they will exploit you with deceptive words" (2 Peter 2:1–3 NKJV).

2. There would be wars, increased seismic activity, food shortages, and widespread disease: "Nation will rise against nation, and kingdom against kingdom. And there will be famines, pestilences, and earthquakes in various places" (Matthew 24:7 NKJV).

3. The moon would become blood red: "The sun shall be turned into darkness, and the moon into blood, before the coming of the great and awesome day of the Lord" (Acts 2:20 NKJV).

4. People would become selfish, materialistic, and blasphemous: "In the last days perilous times will come: for men will be lovers of themselves, lovers of money, boasters, proud, blasphemers" (2 Timothy 3:1–2).

5. The world would embrace homosexuality as a normal lifestyle: "Likewise as it was also in the days of Lot. . . . on the day that Lot went out of Sodom it rained fire and brimstone from heaven and destroyed them all. Even so will it be in the day when the Son of Man is revealed" (Luke 17:28–29). Some believe that Sodom was judged because of their inhospitality. However, the Bible makes it clear that Sodom was given over to homosexuality. The Scriptures say that Lot was "oppressed by the sensual conduct of unprincipled men." These people were "those who indulge[d] the flesh in its corrupt desires and despise[d] authority" (2 Peter 2:7–10 NASB). Jude 7 warns "Sodom and Gomorrah . . . having given themselves over to sexual immorality and gone after strange flesh, are set forth as an example, suffering the vengeance of eternal fire" (NKJV).

6. Religious hypocrisy would be prevalent: "For [although] they hold a form of piety (true religion), they deny and reject and are strangers to the power of it [their conduct belies the genuineness of their profession]" (2 Timothy 3:5 AMP).

7. Men would deny that God created the heavens, and that He destroyed the world through Noah's flood: "There shall come in the last days scoffers. . . . For this they willingly are ignorant of, that by the word of God the heavens were of old, and the earth standing out of the water and in the water: whereby the world that then was, being overflowed with water, perished" (2 Peter 3:3, 5–6).

8. The future would become frightening: ". . . men's hearts failing them from fear and the expectation of those things which are coming on the earth, for the powers of the heavens will be shaken" (Luke 21:26 NKJV).

9. Skeptics (motivated by the sin of lust) would mock these signs, claiming they have always been around: "Scoffers will come in the last days, walking according to their own lusts, and saying, 'Where is the promise of His coming? For since the fathers fell asleep, all things continue as they were from the beginning of creation'" (2 Peter 3:3–4 NKJV).

10. The city of Jerusalem is pivotal in Bible prophecy. Scripture says that it would become a major political problem for the nations: "And it shall happen in that day that I will make Jerusalem a very heavy stone for all peoples" (Zechariah 12:3 NKJV). The powerful Arab nations want to annihilate the nation of Israel, so that they can have Jerusalem as their center of worship. Jesus said, "Jerusalem shall be trodden down of the Gentiles, until the times of the Gentiles be fulfilled" (Luke 21:24). Jerusalem was controlled by the Gentiles (non-Jewish nations) until 1967, when the Jews took its possession. For the first time in two thousand years the Jews stepped into Jerusalem. This sign shows us where we are on the prophetic clock. We are living on the very edge of the coming of God's kingdom—when His will, will be done on earth, as it is in heaven. The tragedy, however, is that despite these evident signs, most will ignore the warning to get right with God.[3]

No other book has these signs of the end of the age, and no other generation had what we have in this generation—the Jews in Jerusalem. You couldn't want better evidence that the Bible is the Word of the Creator than the fulfillment of its age-old prophecies right in front of your eyes.

THE EXISTENCE OF THE SOUL

Professor Dawkins says, "No serious scientist doubts that we are cousins of gorillas, we are cousins of monkeys, we are cousins of snails; we are cousins of earthworms."[4] The word "serious" is supposed to give scientific credibility to a theory that has no scientific basis. This tactic is known as a "logical fallacy," and is specifically called a "no true Scotsman fallacy," which I introduced in chapter 1.[5] If Mr. Dawkins took the time to look around, he would find that there are many credentialed scientists who reject the theory of evolution.[6] If he wants to play the numbers game by saying what many atheists say—that *thousands* of scientists believe in evolution, there are *millions* who believe in creationism—doctors, lawyers, politicians, dentists, computer technicians, engineers, architects, schoolteachers, accountants, and a million and one other professionals. We win.

Even so, he not only believes that we are cousins of worms and snails but that we are cousins of bananas: "It is a plain truth that we are cousins of chimpanzees, somewhat more distant cousins of monkeys, more distant cousins still of aardvarks and manatees, yet more distant cousins of bananas and turnips."[7] But he's wrong. You are not an animal or a cousin of the banana. You are a moral creation, made by God with a sense of justice, truth, and righteousness. That's what separates us from the animals. You are *special* in creation. You are loved by your Creator, who will have no pleasure in your death or damnation.

Professor Dawkins exhorts his fellow "believers" with, "If you're an atheist, you believe this is the only life you're going to get. It's a precious life. It's a beautiful life. It's something we should live to the full, to the end of our days."[8] While it is a beautiful life, he's wrong again about it being finite. Your days are not going to end.

In 2011, I interviewed an evolutionary biologist at UCLA. When I mentioned the "soul," he said that there was no such thing. But when I said, "Do you know that the word 'soul' and the word 'life' are synonymous in the Bible?" he said, "I didn't know that. I believe in the soul, then."

Even when I was a small child, I was the same person I am today. My body is radically different in many ways. My bones, muscles, and brain are larger. My voice is deeper. I look completely different. It's not the same body I had as a small child. Richard Dawkins says the same thing about the radical change of the body:

> Think of an experience from your childhood. Something you remember clearly, something you can see, feel, maybe even smell, as if you were really there. After all you really were there at the time, weren't you? How else could you remember it? But here is the bombshell: you

weren't there. Not a single atom that is in your body today was there when that event took place. . . . Matter flows from place to place and momentarily comes together to be you. Whatever you are, therefore, you are not the stuff of which you are made. If that does not make the hair stand up on the back of your neck, read it again until it does, because it is important.[9]

But look at his conclusion. He says, "You weren't there." The professor doesn't believe that you are more than the atoms of your body. You are just meat, blood, and bone. He doesn't believe that you have life in your body. But the Bible says differently. It tells us that your *soul* is the real you. Your body is merely the temporal housing in which you live. That will change in appearance, but the only difference in your soul is that you will have gained knowledge and experience. Your soul—the real you—is what the Bible says is eternal, and that's what will leave your body at death. If he fails to repent and trust in Jesus, Richard Dawkins will pass on, and in doing so get the shock of his death.

Christians believe that God made man from soil. How dumb is that? If you just said an atheist amen to the dumb question, then I'd like you to do something the next time you go shopping in a supermarket. Look at every food item and ask yourself whether or not it traces itself back to soil: potato chips, milk, cheese, eggs, butter, pancakes, bananas, bread, cookies, grapes, apples, beef, chicken, lamb, pork, popcorn, chocolate, cereal, coffee, strawberries, etc. It takes a little bit of backward thinking, but if you take the time to give it some thought, everything traces itself back to the soil. Let's do it with eggs. The eggs came from the chicken. The chicken ate the wheat to make the eggs, and the wheat traces itself back to the soil. When you were a toddler, your mother gave you milk that came from the cow that chewed the grass that came from the soil. Stated simplistically, milk is rearranged soil nutrients. So are cheese, butter, yogurt and ice cream. The substance of our bodies is made up of the food we eat, and all the food we eat traces itself back to the soil (Mother Earth). We are rearranged dirt. Coincidentally, science tells us that the same trace elements that make up soil also make up the human body—carbon, hydrogen, nitrogen, calcium, and phosphorus. When you die, your body will turn back into soil, and your soiled soul (if you are not trusting in Jesus) will return to the God you don't believe in.

Your soul is the most precious thing you have. Would you sell your eyes for ten million dollars? No one in his right mind would. So how much more is your life worth? It's without price, and you are selling it in exchange for the fleeting pleasures of sin. Your choice right now is that you can either temporarily enjoy fornication, lust, pornography, pride, blasphemy, and rebellion against the God who so graciously gave you the gift of life, and end damned without a hope in hell; or you can, with the help of God, repent and put your faith in Jesus, and enjoy everlasting pleasure.

My heart breaks at what Richard Dawkins has done to the youth of the United States. He's like an eloquent televangelist, with hundreds of thousands of young people who sit at his feet and soak in every word he says, as though it were gospel truth. But it's not. It's based on error, willful ignorance, confusion, and misrepresentation about who God is and what the Bible teaches. Instead of going to another country and destroying the faith of those who are told to love their enemies, he should be trying to fight against militant Islam that is taking over his own country. To resist Islam in England would take great courage, but it wouldn't be as popular or as lucrative as what he does here in the United States. I say with all due respect, Professor Dawkins, go back to your own country and clean up your own backyard. And stop poisoning our youth against the only thing that can save them from impending death and a very real hell.

TOO GOOD TO BE TRUE

The Bible tells us that God's kingdom is coming to this earth, and that His will shall be done on earth as it is in heaven. That means no more disease, fear, pain, suffering, and death. Those who love

God will be given ageless bodies, and the Scriptures tell us that we will have pleasure forevermore. Does this sound too good to be true? It would be if it was promised by some politician. But it's not. This is promised by our faithful Creator, who cannot lie. We do have a problem, though. The Bible tells us that all this will be so incredible we cannot begin to imagine what He has in store for those who love Him (1 Corinthians 2:9). But I have some thoughts that may help a little.

Imagine that you were there "in the beginning," moments before God thundered, "Let there be light." He turns to you and asks if you can imagine what He is going to do over the next six days. You draw a blank. You have no idea what is about to take place. You don't think of breathtaking sunrises and beautiful sunsets, full moons, glittering stars, crystal clear blue water teeming with colorful fish, a myriad of radiant flowers, amazing hummingbirds, the brilliance of the sun, the white sands and tall palm trees on beautiful beaches, massive snowcapped mountains, cascading waterfalls, or eagles flying across the sky-blue heavens. You don't think of a favorite dessert, or satisfying drink, or incredible music, or the most mouthwatering chocolate that ever touched human lips. Neither can you begin to imagine that He is going to make massive animals with five-foot noses and three-foot ears, or tall yellow-and-black patchwork beasts with six-foot-long necks, or bouncy creatures that have a front pocket. You don't visualize the faces of the cutest kittens, or adorable wobbly puppies, or huge whales leaping out of the ocean. You can't conceive of even one of these things because you, too, are just part of God's amazing creation.

Now back in reality, we can see around us what God has created. However, all of this marvelously breathtaking beauty is part of what the Bible calls a "fallen" creation. It is under the Genesis curse of disease, decay, and death. Nothing is as good as it should be. So take all these amazing things we have talked about and drop them all in a big old trash bin, because they are but rotten garbage compared to what God has in store for those who love him.

If you have managed to make it to this point of the book and you're still not a Christian because you have perhaps been influenced by this misguided man Dawkins, please, soften your heart and think on these sobering words from Mark 8:36 (NKJV):

> What will it profit a man if he gains the whole world, and loses his own soul?

Chapter 10
THE EMPEROR HAS NO CLONES

In an interview titled "Was God not the universal architect?" cosmologist Lawrence Krauss excitedly explained the plausibility that the universe wasn't God's creation. A wide-eyed, almost childlike Krauss said that science had found that everything was created from nothing. It was as though the discovery were something new, when that's exactly what the Bible has said for more than three thousand years. God made everything from nothing.

But Krauss then jumped from everything was created from nothing, to nothing created everything. Everything was made *from* nothing doesn't mean that everything was made *by* nothing. The first is good solid science, while the second is a scientific impossibility. He said:

> It's plausible that it was created without God. . . . That's what's worth celebrating. . . . We don't know all the answers, and I don't claim we know all the answers. . . . The laws of nature . . . have created everything we see [in the universe] from nothing. . . . We don't need any supernatural miracles to create everything we see. . . . There's no evidence for God. . . . I can't say with absolute certainty that there is no God, but what I would say is that I much prefer to live in a universe without one.[1]

Saying that Leonardo de Vinci started with a clean canvas is not the same as saying that the *Mona Lisa* painted itself, starting with no paint, brush, or canvas. Yet the smiling interviewer didn't notice what Krauss was saying, and tossed him softball after softball that he hit out of the park for unthinking viewers. He was using the fast-talking, don't-think deeply-about-what-I'm-saying principle so often used by many who embrace atheism. Richard Dawkins used this tactic when he once asked the loaded question, "Why would an all-powerful Creator decide to plant his carefully crafted species on islands and continents in exactly the appropriate pattern to suggest, irresistibly, that they had evolved and dispersed from the site of their evolution?"[2]

Dawkins's question comes pre-packed with suppositions that have no basis in truth. There is no "pattern" to suggest evolution anywhere. Everything is as it is because God created it as it is. God made dogs as dogs, birds as birds, cats and cats, and people as people. To see evolution in all of nature as the professor does is like seeing the Virgin Mary's face in a pizza, on tree stumps, in shadows on walls, and in the big, puffy clouds. You will find her everywhere if you have half a mind to do so. Richard Dawkins has reproduced many "believers" in his own image. They don't have their own thoughts, and instead parrot the professor's anti-Christian words. But on the Day that matters, every person will give an account of himself and herself to God. There will be no clones on Judgment Day. There will be no professor to blame or hide behind.

An atheist named Melissa once wrote in, saying, "Believe it or not, I used to be a Christian." I wrote back:

> I have a question for you, Melissa. Please take a moment to carefully think of the implications before you answer. You said that you "used to be a Christian." So are you therefore saying that you knew the Lord? Is that correct?—because that's the biblical definition of a Christian—to know the Lord. The answer creates a dilemma for someone who believes she is an atheist. If you answer "Yes," then you are admitting, as a professing atheist, that God does exist. So you are forced to default to "I *thought* I did. But I didn't." So you didn't know the Lord. You were never a Christian. You had a false conversion. You are not alone. Millions have had false conversions and they sit in churches faking it. The Bible calls them goats among the sheep (goats in Israel can't be easily distinguished from sheep). You, however, like many other false converts, didn't stay among Christians and fake it for too long. You left church, and became inoculated against the Christianity that you believe didn't deliver its

promises. Almost all in this category are the tragic result of a false gospel and they, like you, have been immunized against the truth. If you would like to know why and how you fell into deception, please take the time to listen to "Hell's Best Kept Secret" and then "True and False Conversion," on www.livingwaters.com. These are free audios.[3]

This is what God's Word says about the atheist and why he or she will be without excuse on Judgment Day:

> For the invisible things of him from the creation of the world are clearly seen, being understood by the things that are made, even His eternal power and Godhead; so that they are without excuse: because that, when they knew God, they glorified him not as God, neither were thankful; but became vain in their imaginations, and their foolish heart was darkened. Professing themselves to be wise, they became fools. (Romans 1:20–22, KJV)

It's amazing how this Bronze-age, "2000-year-old book written by sheepherders"[4] manages to perfectly peg the atheist. An atheist is someone who believes the scientific impossibility that nothing created everything—when the genius of God's creative hand surrounds him. Every atheist knows God exists because of the incredible order of nature, and because He has given them inner light via the conscience (*con* = "with" + *science* = "knowledge"). Yet atheists are unthankful for the gift of life, and imagine that they are primates with no moral responsibility toward their Creator. They darken their own foolish understanding, and then proclaim themselves to be wise. Watch their condescending response and watch them again confirm the truth of Holy Scripture.

Most atheists despise the very thought of "faith," not realizing that they exercise it many times each day. If you want to see some faith in action, watch what happens at the lights at any busy intersection. Drivers speed up to a red light, trusting (having faith) in their brakes. It hardly enters their trusting minds that if the brakes fail, they are almost certainly dead. Watch them take off as soon as the light turns green, again trusting (having faith) that the lights are working correctly, and that the alternative light isn't stuck on green. Their trust (or, faith) is so great that no one is running a red light that they don't even look in that direction to see if the way is clear. Many trusting drivers have taken off in faith, and have tragically gone to meet their Maker. Watch unthinking pedestrians trust (have faith in) the oncoming driver's brakes and his ability to use them, as they step out in front of his car, and trust (have faith in) the lights when they say, "Cross now."

With these thoughts in mind, it's important

to know that when a Christian says to have faith in God, we're not saying to believe that He exists. That's axiomatic. We are saying to exercise the same trust we have each day in things and in people, the difference being that God is utterly faithful because He cannot lie. You can trust Him to never let you down. Ever.

LET'S BELIEVE

Atheists often say that man is the most intellectually evolved among the animals. Okay, let's believe that you are an animal for a moment and that you are more intelligent than the beasts of the earth. I will put aside my thoughts that a man hasn't the intelligence to work out how to fly with the agility of a common sparrow (let alone a hummingbird), or catch a Frisbee in his mouth at six feet, or sniff out a tiny bag of cocaine among airport baggage. I will try to forget that the human race is so senseless that we have devoured hundreds of millions of our fellow animals through war, up to 200 million through genocide, and millions by just plain murdering them. I will try to believe that it wasn't evil—that it was actually wise because it was Darwin's survival of the fittest in action—the strongest and fittest-for-war nations simply overcame the weakest animals and killed or enslaved them.

So let's believe that you are one individual animal among billions. Then, as an animal, listen to your evolution-given instinct to survive. You are cornered by a determined killer. It has the smell of your warm blood in its nostrils. It is salivating at the very thought of slaying you, and it's just a matter of time until it devours you.

Its name is Eternal Justice, and like a furious judge, it will bring down its gavel upon your guilty soul and will justly send you to a terrible place. What are you going to do? Not even a dumb animal would be so deluded as to pretend the predator isn't there. His instinct to survive will kick in and he will run for his very life. *Do that!* Run for your life—to the cross! Run to the Savior, Jesus Christ, and fall at His feet. You have no other hope. You are sitting in the shadow of death. Eternal Justice is robed and waiting for you to plead. What is your plea? You have only one thing you can say if you want to survive: "I am guilty. Have mercy upon me, O God, a sinner!" and He, in His great mercy, will make you fit to survive.

If you have truly repented and trusted in Jesus, please go to www.livingwaters.com and click on "Save Yourself Some Pain." That will help you grow in your newfound faith.

NOTES

Chapter 1

1. Richard Dawkins, Review of *Blueprints: Solving the Mystery of Evolution*, *New York Times*, April 9, 1989, sec. 7, 34.

2. Jonah Lehrer, "Why We Don't Believe in Science," *Frontal Cortex* (*New Yorker* blog), June 7, 2012, www. newyorker.com/online/blogs/frontal-cortex/2012/06/ brain-experiments-why-we-dont-believe-science.html.

3. Ibid.

4. "'We are Distant Cousins to Bananas and Turnips' Says Richard Dawkins," a review of Richard Dawkins's *The Greatest Show on Earth: The Evidence for Evolution*, (New York: Free Press, 2010), 8; posted April 7, 2011, on the website of Creation Revolution, http:// creationrevolution.com/2011/04/%e2%80%98we-are- distant-cousins-to-bananas-and-turnips%e2%80%99- says-richard-dawkins/#ixzz2BF0NUXuS.

5. This tactic—saying that "all respectable, intelligent, sane people" believe a certain thing—is known as a *logical fallacy*, and is specifically called a "no true Scotsman fallacy." See *Wikipedia*, s.v. "No true Scotsman," http:// en.wikipedia.org/wiki/No_true_Scotsman.

6. Laura Sheahen, "The Problem with God: Interview with Richard Dawkins," beliefnet, http://www.beliefnet.com/ News/Science-Religion/2005/11/The-Problem-With- God-Interview-With-Richard-Dawkins.aspx?p=2.

7. "Misconceptions about evolution," Understanding Evolution, University of California Museum of Paleontology, August 22, 2008, http://evolution.berkeley. edu/evolibrary/misconceptions_faq.php#e1.

8. Ibid.

9. "Tailbone," Laser Spine Institute webpage, http://www. laserspineinstitute.com/back_problems/spinal_anatomy/ tailbone/.

10. Duke Medicine News and Communications, "Appendix Isn't Useless at All: It's a Safe House for Bacteria," DukeHealth.org, http://www.dukehealth.org/health_library/news/10151.

11. See https://www.facebook.com/official.Ray.Comfort.

12. "Genetic, fossil and archaeological evidence have now demonstrated that all humans share a common ancestor." Jay T. Stock, "Are humans still evolving?" EMBO *Reports* 9 (suppl. 1) (July 2008): S51–S54, http://www.ncbi.nlm.nih.gov/pmc/articles/PMC3327538/.

13. National Institutes of Health, "Deoxyribonucleic Acid (DNA)," genome.gov, upd. June 13, 2012, http://www.genome.gov/25520880. Courtesy: National Human Genome Research Institute.

14. Stock, "Are humans still evolving?"

Chapter 2

1. Walkie-talkie, s.v. "Richard Dawkins," http://en.wikiquote.org/wiki/Richard_Dawkins.

2. "Professor Richard Dawkins on Darwin," National Geographic Channel website, http://natgeotv.com/uk/dawkins-darwin-evolution/dawkins-interview-darwin.

3. Ibid.

4. Ibid.

5. *Wikipedia*, s.v. "Carl Sagan," http://en.wikipedia.org/wiki/Carl_Sagan.

6. It was atheist Clarence Darrow who similarly said, "I don't believe in God because I don't believe in Mother Goose." (*Wikipedia*, s.v. "Clarence Darrow," http://en.wikiquote.org/wiki/Clarence_Darrow).

7. See https://www.facebook.com/official.Ray.Comfort, February 2, 2013.

8. "Natural selection and evolution: Theories of evolution—higher," Bitesize (Science),

9. http://www.bbc.co.uk/schools/gcsebitesize/science/ocr_gateway_pre_2011/environment/4_survival_of_fittest6.shtml, p. 6.

10. Ibid.

11. "We seldom realise that we *are* apes," http://old. richarddawkins.net/quotes/14; see also http://www. theguardian.com/science/dawkins.

12. Check out their comments at http://www.amazon. com/Lead-Atheist-Evidence-Cant-Think/product- reviews/1935071068/ref=dp_top_cm_cr_acr_ txt?ie=UTF8&showViewpoints=1.

Chapter 3

1. Paul Bond, "Hollywood's Top 10 Atheists," Newsmax, http://w3.newsmax.com/a/athiests/.

2. Billy Joel, on Quotes, http://www.quotes.net/ quote/14538.

3. "Brad Pitt on Atheism & Hatred: Star Talks God, Genocide And Inequality," *Huffington Post* Entertainment, January 25, 2012, http://www. huffingtonpost.com/2012/01/25/brad-pitt-on-atheism- hatr_n_1231684.html.

4. Gina Salamone, "Brad Pitt: 'I'm probably 20 percent atheist and 80 percent agnostic,'" *Daily News*, July 23, 2009, http://www.nydailynews.com/entertainment/ gossip/brad-pitt-20-percent-atheist-80-percent-agnostic- article-1.394661#ixzz2BkBiqx4O.

5. David Brewster, *A Short Scheme of the True Religion, manuscript quoted in Memoirs of the Life, Writings and Discoveries of Sir Isaac Newton* (Edinburgh, 1850), quoted in *Newton's Philosophy of Nature: Selections from his writings*, ed. H. S. Thayer (New York: Hafner Library of Classics, 1953), 65.

6. "Brad Pitt on Atheism & Hatred."

7. "Quote of the Day: Brad Pitt on God," *I'm Not Obsessed* (blog), May 19, 2011, http://www.imnotobsessed. com/2011/05/19/quote-of-the-day-brad-pitt-on-god/#. ULKng4dWxI4.

8. Joshua M. Greene, "George Harrison—Beatle, Seeker, Lover of God," on the Joshua M. Green *Yogesvara* website, http://www.atma.org/media-2/articles/george- harrison/.

9. Geoffrey Giuliano, *Dark Horse: The Life and Art of George Harrison*, upd. ed. (Boston: Da Capo Press, 1997), 99.

10. 10. "Top 10 George Carlin Quotes," *Alternative Reel*, http://www.alternativereel.com/soc/display_article.php?id=0000000019.

11. Ibid.

12. Penn Jillette, "There Is No God," NPR, November 21, 2005, http://www.npr.org/2005/11/21/5015557/there-is-no-god.

13. F.H. Bradley, as quoted in *Between System and Poetics: William Desmond and Philosophy After Dialectic*, Thomas A.F. Kelly, ed. (Farnham, Surrey, UK: Ashgate, 2007), 41.

14. Jillette, "There Is No God."

15. Ibid.

16. Ibid.

17. Rebecca Keegan, *The Futurist: The Life and Films of James Cameron*, Google eBook (New York: Random House, 2009), chap. 1.

18. Roger Ebert, "I do not fear death," *Salon*, September 15, 2011, http://www.salon.com/2011/09/15/roger_ebert/.

19. Ibid.

20. Ibid.

21. Bill Foster, *Meet the Skeptic: A Field Guide to Faith Conversations*, Google eBook (Green Forest, AR: New Leaf, 2012).

22. Cal Fussman, "Jodie Foster: What I've Learned," *Esquire*, December 14, 2010, http://www.esquire.com/features/what-ive-learned/meaning-of-life-2011/jodie-foster-interview-0111#ixzz2BkHBXWec.

23. *Wikipedia*, s.v. "Jodie Foster," http://en.wikipedia.org/wiki/Jodie_Foster.

24. "Jodie Foster's 'Coming Out Speech' at 2013 Golden Globes, *Vibe*, January 14, 2013, http://www.vibe.com/article/jodie-fosters-coming-out-speech-2013-golden-globes.

25. David J. Stewart, "Hugh Hefner a Moral Guy?" JesusisSavior.com, http://www.jesus-is-savior.com/Evils%20in%20America/Porno/hugh_hefner.htm.

26. Celebrity Atheist List, http://www.celebatheists.
com/wiki/Steve_Jobs; but see search results for
"Steve Jobs an atheist" at https://www.google.com/
webhp?source=search_app#hl=en&gs_rn=7&gs_ri=psy-
ab&gs_mss=steve%20Jobs%20an%20a&tok=BQ0OLM
20vqrU2GIsZtBPYg&cp=21&gs_id=2c&xhr=t&q=steve
+jobs+an+atheist&es_nrs=true&pf=p&output=search&s
client=psy-ab&rlz=1C2GGGE_enUS458US458&oq=ste
ve+Jobs+an+atheist&gs_l=&pbx=1&bav=on.2,or.r_cp.r_
qf.&bvm=bv.44158598,d.cGE&fp=897ba9997041d6f1
&biw=2239&bih=1211.

27. NPR staff, "New Bio Quotes Jobs on God, Gates and
Great Design," NPR, October 25, 2011, http://www.npr.
org/2011/10/25/141656955/new-bio-quotes-jobs-on-
god-gates-and-great-design.

28. "1980 Playboy Interview with John Lennon
And Yoko Ono," http://www.john-lennon.com/
playboyinterviewwithjohnlennonandyokoono.htm.

29. David Sheff, *All We Are Saying: The Last Major Interview
with John Lennon and Yoko Ono*, first St. Martin's Griffin
ed. (New York: St. Martin's Press, 2000), 212.

30. Joel Whitburn, *Top Pop Singles 1955–2002* (Record
Research, 2002), 382.

Chapter 4

1. Steven Salzburg, "Evolution bugs people," *Forbes*,
March 11, 2012, http://www.forbes.com/sites/
stevensalzberg/2012/03/11/evolution-bugs-people/.

2. Ibid.

3. From "Are We Related?" *Simply Heavenly Food* (blog),
January 12, 2013, http://simplyheavenlyfood.tumblr.
com/post/40369040298/jim-cockman-said-bonobos-are-
our-closest-dna.

4. Jesse Ventura on *Piers Morgan Tonight*, September 22,
2012, as quoted on CNN's transcript posted at http://
transcripts.cnn.com/TRANSCRIPTS/1209/22/pmt.01.
html.

5. See http://thinkexist.com/quotation/sir-my_concern_ is_not_whether_god_is_on_our_side/164075.html. See also Leon G. Stevens, One Nation Under God: A Factual History of America's Religious Heritage: From Our Founding Fathers Until Today and Beyond (Nashville, TN: WestBow Press, 2012), 129.

6. Mark Twain's Notebook, 1902–1903; William E. Phipps, Mark Twain's Religion (Macon, GA: Mercer University Press, 2003), 276.

7. See http://thinkexist.com/quotation/the_longer_i_live-the_more_convincing_proofs_i/261270.html; William Makepeace Thayer, The printer boy: or, How Ben Franklin made his mark. An example for youth (n.p.: Ulan Press, 2012; manuscript notes from Franklin's speech at the Constitutional Convention (June 28, 1787), preserved in the Library of Congress, and available for view at http://www.loc.gov/exhibits/religion/ vc006642.jpg.

8. "A Founding Father's view of God," Los Angeles Times, July 5, 2008, http://articles.latimes.com/2008/jul/05/ local/me-beliefs5; Thomas Jefferson, The Works of Thomas Jefferson: Correspondence and Papers, 1816–1826 (n.p.: Cosimo Classics, 2010).

9. Transcript of recovered FBI tape Q 622, available to view on the website of the Jonestown Institute, at http://www-rohan.sdsu.edu/~remoore/jonestown/AboutJonestown/ Tapes/Tapes/TapeTranscripts/Q622.html.

10. Quote taken from an interview with Stone Phillips, Dateline NBC, November 29, 1994.

Chapter 5

1. Celebrity Atheist List, http://www.celebatheists. com/wiki/Thomas_Edison; see also http://www. positiveatheism.org/hist/edison.htm; http://atheism. about.com/library/quotes/bl_q_TAEdison.htm.

2. As quoted in The Romance and Drama of the Rubber Industry (1936) by Harvey Samuel Firestone.

3. Christopher Hitchens, God Is Not Great: How Religion Poisons Everything (New York: Random House, 2008), 64.

4. Celebrity Atheist List, http://www.celebatheists.com/wiki/Bill_Gates.

5. "The Generous Atheist Billionaires," *Patheos* (blog), October 28, 2010, http://www.patheos.com/blogs/friendlyatheist/2010/10/28/the-generous-atheist-billionaires/.

6. "Bill Gates interview: I have no use for money. This is God's work," *Telegraph* (UK), January 18, 2013, http://www.telegraph.co.uk/technology/bill-gates/9812672/Bill-Gates-interview-I-have-no-use-for-money.-This-is-Gods-work.html.

7. Einstein "God Letter" Sold on eBay for Just over $3 Million," Richard Dawkins Foundation, posted October 25, 2012, http://richarddawkins.net/news_articles/2012/10/25/einstein-god-letter-sold-on-ebay-for-just-over-3-million#.UJjsLcVWxI4.

8. Jessica Ravitz, "Einstein letter, set for auction, shows scientist challenging idea of God, being 'chosen,'" *Belief* (CNN blog), October 4, 2012, http://religion.blogs.cnn.com/2012/10/04/einstein-letter-set-for-auction-shows-scientist-challenging-idea-of-god-being-chosen/?hpt=hp_c2.

9. Albert Einstein, letter to Guy H. Raner Jr., September 28, 1949, quoted by Michael R. Gilmore in *Skeptic* 5, no. 2 (1997).

10. Hubertus zu Löwenstein, *Towards the Further Shore: An Autobiography* (London: Victor Gollancz, 1968), 156.

11. Richard Dawkins, *The God Delusion* (London: Transworld, 2006), 34.

12. George Sylvester Viereck, *Glimpses of the Great* (London: Duckworth, 1930).

13. Walter Isaacson, "Einstein & Faith," *Time*, April 5, 2007, http://www.time.com/time/magazine/article/0,9171,1607298,00.html#ixzz28b9PxWLC.

14. Richard Dawkins, "Albert Einstein's Historic 1954 "God Letter," Richard Dawkins, September 17, 2012, http://richarddawkins.net/news_articles/2012/8/15/albert-einstein-s-historic-1954-god-letter-handwritten-shortly-before-his-death.

15. Darwin Online, excerpted from Francis Darwin, ed., *The life and letters of Charles Darwin, including an autobiographical chapter*, vol. 1 (London: John Murray, 1887), 305, http://darwin-online.org.uk/content/framese t?pageseq=1&itemID=F1452.1&viewtype=text.

16. Jeffrey Meyers, *Hemingway: A Biography* (Boston: Da Capo, 1985), 560–561.

Chapter 6

1. Nicole Menzie, "British Atheist Richard Dawkins Explores Sin and Morality in New TV Series," *Christian Post*, October 17, 2012, http://www.christianpost.com/ news/british-atheist-richard-dawkins-explores-sin-and-morality-in-new-tv-series-83113/.

2. *Dictionary.com Unabridged*, s.v. "good," Random House, Inc., http://dictionary.reference.com/browse/good; accessed January 30, 2014.

3. Ibid., s.v. "sin."

Chapter 7

4. PZ Meyers, "What are you an atheist?" *Science Blogs: Pharyngula*, February 1, 2011, http://scienceblogs.com/ pharyngula/2011/02/why_are_you_an_atheist.php.

5. Ibid.

6. Ibid.

7. Ibid.

8. Frederic P. Miller, Agnes F. Vandome, and McBrewster John, eds., *Expelled: No Intelligence Allowed* (Beau-Bassin, Mauritius: Alphascript, 2010).

9. Steve Paulson, "The Flying Spaghetti Monster," *Salon*, October 13, 2006, http://www.salon.com/2006/10/13/ dawkins_3/.

10. Meyers, "What are you an atheist?"

11. Ibid.

12. Alejandra Molina, "Bicyclist hit twice by vehicles dies," *Orange County Register*, December 23, 2010, http://www. ocregister.com/news/brookhurst-281480-ankenbrand-beach.html.

Chapter 8

1. CBS News, "Bill Nye on creationism critique: I'm not attacking religion," from the website of *CBS This Morning*, August 28, 2012, www.cbsnews.com/8301-505270_162-57501492/bill-nye-on-creationism-critique-im-not-attacking-religion/.

2. Ibid.

3. John R. Vile, *The Constitutional Convention of 1787: A Comprehensive Encyclopedia of America's Founding*, vol. 1 (Santa Barbara, CA: ABC-CLIO, 2005), 593.

4. Carver is quoted as saying, "I never have to grope for methods. The method is revealed at the moment I am inspired to create something new. Without God to draw aside the curtain I would be helpless." W.J. Federer, *America's God and Country Encyclopedia of Quotations* (Coppell, TX: FAME, 1994), 96.

5. "Buzz Aldrin's Communion on the Moon," a video submitted to YouTube by Rodion Herrera, on July 14, 2009, http://www.youtube.com/watch?v=5zEZvPg1itw&feature=related.

6. "Faith and the Bible in the Apollo Moon Program," *Classical Astronomy* (newsletter), http://www.classicalastronomy.com/news/anmviewer.asp?a=316&.

7. "Apollo 8 – Book of Genesis Reading (December 24, 1968)," a video submitted to YouTube by TheApollo11Channel, September 2, 2010, http://www.youtube.com/watch?v=njpWalYduU4.

8. Lona Manning, "The Murder of Madalyn Murray O'Hair: America's Most Hated Woman," *Crime* magazine, upd. September 23, 2003, http://crimemagazine.com/murder-madalyn-murray-ohair-americas-most-hated-woman-1.

Chapter 9

1. Richard Dawkins, *The God Delusion*, repr. ed. (Boston: Mariner, 2008), 256.

2. Ibid.

3. See my book *Scientific Facts in the Bible: 100 Reasons to Believe the Bible is Supernatural in Origin* (Gainesville, FL: Bridge-Logos, 2001).

4. Hemant Mehta, "Richard Dawkins: 'Who Cares About Creationists? They Don't Know Anything'" *The Friendly Atheist* (Patheos blog), September 7, 2012, http://www.patheos.com/blogs/friendlyatheist/2012/09/07/richard-dawkins-who-cares-about-creationists-they-dont-know-anything/.

5. See *Wikipedia*, s.v. "No true Scotsman," http://en.wikipedia.org/wiki/No_true_Scotsman.

6. *A Scientific Dissent from Darwinism*, upd. July 2013, discovery.org/scripts/viewDB/filesDB-download.php?command=download&id=660.

7. Richard Dawkins, *The Greatest Show on Earth*, repr. ed. (New York: Free Press, 2010).

8. You can hear him make this statement on several YouTube videos.

9. Dawkins, *The God Delusion*.

Chapter 10

1. CNN, September 24, 2012, http://www.cnn.com/video/?utm_source=feedburner&utm_medium=feed&utm_campaign=Feed%3A+rss%2Fcnn_topstories+%28RSS%3A+Top+Stories%29#/video/living/2012/09/24/intv-krauss-universe-nothing.cnn.

2. Richard Dawkins, *The Greatest Show on Earth*.

3. "Words of Comfort: Goats among the Sheep," *The Comfort Zone*, March 27, 2013, http://www.onthebox.us/2013/03/words-of-comfort-goats-among-sheep.html.

4. Comment from "Melissa" posted July 17, 2013, in response to Dan Merica's article "Behold, the six types of atheists" on CNN's *Belief Blog*, July 15, 2013, http://religion.blogs.cnn.com/2013/07/15/the-six-types-of-atheists/comment-page-65/.

For a complete list of books, tracts,
audios, and videos by Ray Comfort go
to: www.livingwaters.com

"The Consummate Apologetics Bible...
Everything you ever need to share your faith."

"The Evidence Bible *is the reservoir overflowing with everything evangelistic—powerful quotes from famous people, amazing anecdotes, sobering last words, informative charts, and a wealth of irrefutable evidence to equip, encourage, and enlighten you, like nothing else.*

I couldn't recommend it more highly."
– Kirk Cameron

Compiled by Ray Comfort

This edition of *The Evidence Bible* includes notes, commentaries, and quotations that make it a comprehensive work of apologetics and evangelism that will be helpful to every believer. It covers a variety of practical topics, including the following:

- How to answer objections to Christianity
- How to talk about Christ with people of other religions
- How to counter evolutionary theories, while providing evidence for God's creation
- How to grow in Christ
- How to use the Ten Commandments when witnessing

There is no other Bible like this one. Every soul-winner who wants to lead others to Christ will want a copy of *The Evidence Bible*, because it provides springboards for preaching and witnessing, shares insights from well-known Christian leaders, gives points for open-air preaching, reveals the scientific facts contained within the Bible, and supplies the believer with helpful keys to sharing one's faith. The Bible is "the sword of the Spirit," and this edition of the Bible will motivate believers to become true spiritual warriors in their daily interactions with others.

THE
EVIDENCE
BIBLE _NKJV_

All You Need to Understand and Defend Your Faith

COMMENTARY BY
RAY COMFORT

ISBN: 9780882705255
PB

_Also available in
duo tone leather._

ISBN: 9780882708973

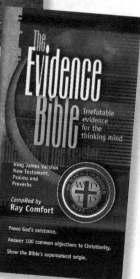

The
Evidence
Bible

irrefutable
evidence
for the
thinking mind

King James Version
New Testament,
Psalms and
Proverbs

Compiled by
Ray Comfort

Prove God's existence.

Answer 100 common objections to Christianity.

Show the Bible's supernatural origin.

The Best of Ray

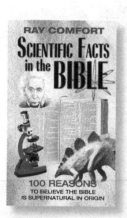

Scientific Facts in the Bible
Ray Comfort

Explore a wealth of incredible scientific, medical, and prophetic facts.

978-0-88270-879-9
MM / 104 pages

The Way of the Master
Ray Comfort and Kirk Cameron

A proven and effective way of making the gospel make sense to the unsaved. Learn how to speak directly to the conscience in the same way Jesus did.

978-0-88270-220-9
TPB / 368 pages